150 BAKING *recipes*
INSPIRED IDEAS FOR EVERYDAY COOKING

150 CAKE *recipes*
INSPIRED IDEAS FOR EVERYDAY COOKING

150 CHICKEN *recipes*
INSPIRED IDEAS FOR EVERYDAY COOKING

150 CUPCAKE & MUFFIN *recipes*
INSPIRED IDEAS FOR EVERYDAY COOKING

150 FAST & SIMPLE *recipes*
INSPIRED IDEAS FOR EVERYDAY COOKING

150 INDIAN *recipes*
INSPIRED IDEAS FOR EVERYDAY COOKING

150 PASTA *recipes*
INSPIRED IDEAS FOR EVERYDAY COOKING

150 SLOW COOKER *recipes*
INSPIRED IDEAS FOR EVERYDAY COOKING

150 STIR-FRY *recipes*
INSPIRED IDEAS FOR EVERYDAY COOKING

150 STUDENT *recipes*
INSPIRED IDEAS FOR EVERYDAY COOKING

150 TAPAS *recipes*
INSPIRED IDEAS FOR EVERYDAY COOKING

150 VEGETARIAN *recipes*
INSPIRED IDEAS FOR EVERYDAY COOKING

D0418704

150

GRANDMA'S
recipes

INSPIRED IDEAS FOR
EVERYDAY COOKING

CONTENTS

INTRODUCTION

Looking back at those precious times spent with Grandma in the kitchen undoubtedly evokes some wonderful memories from the past, especially when it involved rustling up some truly delicious homemade goodies. Those fond childhood memories of Grandma leafing through her old recipes snipped from magazines, or just scribbled down on a piece of paper and slotted into a binder or book, can now be recreated with our myriad of moreish recipes from days gone by.

This savvy selection of mouthwatering recipes includes an amazing array of fabulous family recipes all inspired by Grandma's finest collection, featuring flavourful fuss-free midweek meals or suppers, as well as some

more elaborate eats, perfect for a family celebration or special occasion.

With this inspirational cookbook showcasing a comprehensive collection of traditional recipes, you can now create many of Grandma's everyday favourites at home for your own family to feast on, thus ensuring that these time-honoured dishes can be enjoyed by many generations to come.

We begin our culinary journey down memory lane with a wonderful collection of Grandma's classic favourites, including hearty stews, pies and puddings, as well as classic cakes, cookies and desserts. Focus on family favourites like Shepherd's

Pie, Toad in the Hole or Sausages & Mash with Onion Gravy, or choose from delicious easy eats like Ploughman's Lunch, Fish & Chips with Mushy Peas or Colcannon. Tempting bakes include Irish Soda Bread and Classic Chocolate Cake, or enjoy some vintage nursery puddings like Spotted Dick, Jam Roly-Poly or Rice Pudding.

Next up we concentrate on comforting homely dishes, all guaranteed to banish the blues and keep chills at bay, many of which are sure to earn a regular slot at your table. Familiar flavour-packed dishes range from soul-warming soups like Leek and Potato Soup or Cream of Tomato Soup, to over popular comfort foods like Luxury Cauliflower Cheese, Beef & Stout Pies or Sausage Rolls, all certain to deliver on flavour. Perfect pasta picks ideal for midweek meals include full-on-flavour Quick Spaghetti Bolognese and Spaghetti Alla Carbonara.

For special family occasions or celebration dinners, we cover a sensational selection of delicious dishes, from pâtès, canapés and gratins, to roasts, risottos and bakes. Meaty mouthfuls include traditional Roast Turkey, Glazed Gammon in Cider and Beef Wellington, or if fish or shellfish takes your fancy, try Poached Salmon, Potted Crab or Cockle & Mussel Gratin. For those who prefer a vegetarian option, inspiring meat-free meals like Pumpkin and Chestnut Risotto or Red Cabbage Stuffed with Mushrooms, Nuts & Rice make the most of versatile vegetables.

Satisfy those sweet cravings in our next chapter, which features a paradise of perfect puddings and sweet treats from Grandma's kitchen. Encompassing a scrumptious selection of hot and cold feel-good favourites, select from delectable delights like Sticky Toffee Pudding, Treacle Tart or Hedgerow Fruit Crumble, or choose chilled desserts such as Irish Whiskey Trifle, boozy Summer Pudding or Gooseberry Fool. Alternatively, treat yourself to some sensational vintage sweet treats like Whisky Fudge, Peanut Brittle, Peppermint Creams or Coconut Ice, just like Grandma used to make.

To complete our collection, the enticing aromas created by our assortment of Grandma's all-time best bakes are sure to tempt your family to the kitchen. Featuring a fantastic variety of the finest cupcakes, biscuits, brownies, muffins, shortbread and scones, plus some home-baked breads and rolls, we include some tasty timeless classics such as Cherry Cake, Iced Madeira Cake and Date & Walnut Loaf. Or why not enjoy munching your way through some brilliant bars and bites like Gingernuts, Custard Tarts, Raspberry Crumble Muffins or Chocolate Caramel Shortbread? Finally, for those who prefer something savoury, prime picks such as Savoury Oat Crackers, Granary Loaf and Seeded Rye Bread are sure to hit the spot.

INTRODUCTION

GRANDMA'S CLASSIC FAVOURITES

HEARTY BEEF STEW

Serves: 4 **Prep: 35 mins** **Cook: 2¼–2½ hours,** plus resting

Ingredients

1.3 kg/3 lb boneless braising steak, cut into 5-cm/2-inch pieces

2 tbsp vegetable oil

2 onions, cut into 2.5-cm/1-inch pieces

3 tbsp plain flour

3 garlic cloves, finely chopped

1 litre/1¾ pints beef stock

3 carrots, cut into 2.5-cm/1-inch lengths

2 celery sticks, cut into 2.5-cm/1-inch lengths

1 tbsp tomato ketchup

1 bay leaf

¼ tsp dried thyme

¼ tsp dried rosemary

900 g/2 lb potatoes, such as Maris Piper, cut into large chunks

salt and pepper

Method

1 Season the steak generously. Heat the oil in a large flameproof casserole over a high heat. When the oil begins to smoke slightly, add the steak, in batches, and cook, stirring frequently, for 5–8 minutes, until well browned. Using a slotted spoon, transfer to a bowl.

2 Reduce the heat to medium, add the onions to the casserole and cook, stirring occasionally, for 5 minutes, until translucent. Stir in the flour and cook, stirring constantly, for 2 minutes. Add the garlic and cook for 1 minute. Whisk in 225 ml/8 fl oz of the stock and cook, scraping up all the sediment from the base of the casserole, then stir in the remaining stock and add the carrots, celery, tomato ketchup, bay leaf, thyme, rosemary and 1 teaspoon of salt. Return the steak to the casserole.

3 Bring back to a gentle simmer, cover and cook over a low heat for 1 hour. Add the potatoes, re-cover the casserole and simmer for 30 minutes. Remove the lid, increase the heat to medium and cook, stirring occasionally, for a further 30 minutes, or until the meat and vegetables are tender. If the stew becomes too thick, add a little more stock or water and adjust the seasoning. Leave to rest for 15 minutes before serving.

★ Variation

For extra flavour and colour garnish with fresh tarragon. Serve with crusty bread for mopping up the stew juices.

GRANDMA'S CLASSIC FAVOURITES

SHEPHERD'S PIE

Serves: 6   **Prep: 30 mins**   **Cook: 1¼-1½ hours**

Ingredients

1 tbsp olive oil

2 onions, finely chopped

2 garlic cloves, finely chopped

675 g/1 lb 8 oz good quality minced lamb

2 carrots, finely chopped

1 tbsp plain flour

225 ml/8 fl oz beef or chicken stock

125 ml/4 fl oz red wine

Worcestershire sauce (optional)

salt and pepper

Mashed potato

675 g/1 lb 8 oz floury potatoes, such as King Edward, Maris Piper or Desirée, cut into chunks

55 g/2 oz butter

2 tbsp single cream or milk

salt and pepper

Method

1 Preheat the oven to 180°C/350°F/Gas Mark 4.

2 Heat the oil in a large saucepan and fry the onion until softened, then add the garlic and stir well. Raise the heat and add the meat. Cook quickly to brown the meat all over, stirring continually. Add the carrots and season with salt and pepper to taste. Stir in the flour and add the stock and wine. Stir well and heat until simmering and thickened.

3 Place the meat mixture in a covered casserole and cook in the oven for about 1 hour. Check the consistency from time to time and add a little more stock or wine if required. The meat mixture should be quite thick but not dry. Season to taste with salt. Add a little Worcestershire sauce, if desired.

4 While the meat is cooking, make the mashed potato. Cook the potatoes in a large saucepan of lightly salted boiling water for 15–20 minutes. Drain and mash with a potato masher until smooth. Add the butter and cream, seasoning with salt and pepper to taste. Spoon the lamb mixture into an ovenproof serving dish and spread or pipe the potato on top.

5 Increase the oven temperature to 200°C/400°F/Gas Mark 6 and cook the pie for a further 15–20 minutes at the top of the oven until golden brown. Serve immediately.

GRANDMA'S CLASSIC FAVOURITES

IRISH SODA BREAD

Makes: 1 loaf

Prep: 20 mins,
plus cooling

Cook: 25–30 mins

Ingredients

vegetable oil, for oiling

450 g/1 lb plain flour,
plus extra for dusting

1 tsp salt

1 tsp bicarbonate of soda

400 ml/14 fl oz buttermilk

Method

1 Preheat the oven to 220°C/425°F/Gas Mark 7. Oil
a baking tray.

2 Sift the flour, salt and bicarbonate of soda into a
mixing bowl. Make a well in the centre of the dry
ingredients and pour in most of the buttermilk.
Mix well together using your hands. The dough
should be very soft but not too wet. If necessary,
add the remaining buttermilk.

3 Turn out the dough onto a lightly floured surface
and knead it lightly. Shape into a 20-cm/8-inch
round.

4 Place the loaf on the prepared baking tray
and cut a cross into the top with a sharp knife.
Bake in the preheated oven for 25–30 minutes,
until golden brown and it sounds hollow when
tapped on the bottom. Transfer to a wire rack
and leave to cool slightly. Serve warm.

APPLE & OATMEAL COOKIES

Makes: 26

Prep: 30 mins,
plus cooling

Cook: 12–15 mins

Ingredients

2 large apples, peeled
and cored (200 g/7 oz
unpeeled weight)

1 tsp lemon juice

225 g/8 oz butter, softened,
plus extra for greasing

100 g/3½ oz soft light
brown sugar

100 g/3½ oz caster sugar

1 egg, beaten

225 g/8 oz self-raising flour

150 g/5½ oz rolled oats

85 g/3 oz raisins

Method

1 Preheat the oven to 180°C/350°F/Gas Mark 4.
Grease three large baking sheets. Finely dice the
apples and toss in the lemon juice.

2 Place the butter, brown sugar and caster sugar in
a bowl and beat together until creamy. Gradually
beat in the egg. Sift in the flour and add the oats,
raisins and apple. Mix until thoroughly combined.

3 Place dessertspoonfuls of the mixture on the
prepared baking sheets, spaced well apart.

4 Bake in the preheated oven for 12–15 minutes,
or until golden around the edges. Leave to cool
on the baking sheets for 5–10 minutes, or until
firm enough to transfer to wire racks to cool
completely.

CLASSIC CHOCOLATE CAKE

Serves: 8

Prep: 30–35 mins, plus cooling

Cook: 25–30 mins

Ingredients

150 g/5½ oz plain white flour

25 g/1 oz cocoa powder

175 g/6 oz golden caster sugar

1 tbsp baking powder

175 g/6 oz unsalted butter, at room temperature, plus extra for greasing

3 eggs beaten

1 tsp vanilla extract

2 tbsp milk

Frosting

115 g/4 oz unsalted butter, at room temperature

200 g/7 oz icing sugar

2 tbsp cocoa powder

1 tsp vanilla extract

Method

1 Preheat the oven to 180°C/350°F/Gas Mark 4. Grease and line the base and sides of two 20-cm/8-inch sandwich cake tins. Sift the flour, cocoa, sugar and baking powder into a large bowl and make a well in the centre.

2 Beat the butter until soft. Add to the dry ingredients with the eggs, vanilla extract and milk. Beat lightly with a wooden spoon until just smooth.

3 Spoon the mixture into the prepared tins, smoothing with a palette knife. Bake in the preheated oven for 25–30 minutes, until risen and firm.

4 Leave the cakes to cool in the tins for 2–3 minutes, then turn out onto a wire rack and leave to cool completely.

5 To make the frosting, beat the butter until smooth and fluffy. Sift the icing sugar with the cocoa and beat into the butter until smooth.

6 Stir in the vanilla extract with enough hot water to mix to a soft spreading consistency.

7 When the cakes are cold, sandwich them together with half the frosting, then spread the remainder over the top, swirling with a palette knife. Cut into slices and serve.

TOAD IN THE HOLE

Serves: 4   **Prep: 20 mins**   **Cook: 35–40 mins**

Ingredients

8 rashers streaky bacon

8 thick pork sausages

175 g/6 oz plain flour

pinch of salt

2 large eggs

150 ml/5 fl oz milk

150 ml/5 fl oz beer

1 tbsp chopped fresh thyme

2 tbsp sunflower oil

onion gravy, to serve (see page 31)

Method

1 Preheat the oven to 220°C/425°F/Gas Mark 7. Wrap a bacon rasher around each sausage and place in a flameproof roasting tin (the tin will need to be approximately 30 cm x 23 cm/12 inches x 9 inches). Bake in the preheated oven for 10 minutes.

2 Place the flour and salt in a bowl. Make a well in the centre and add the eggs, then gradually beat in the milk, followed by the beer, to make a smooth batter. Stir in the thyme. Pour into a jug and set aside.

3 Pour away any watery juices from the roasting tin. Rearrange the sausages, add the oil and heat on the hob until smoking hot. Quickly pour the batter over the sausages and bake in the preheated oven for 25–30 minutes until risen, crisp and golden brown. Serve with gravy.

GRANDMA'S CLASSIC FAVOURITES

LANCASHIRE HOT POT

Serves: 6   **Prep: 30–35 mins**   **Cook: 2½ hours**

Ingredients

900 g/2 lb best end
lamb chops

3 lambs' kidneys,
cored and quartered

55 g/2 oz butter

900 g/2 lb floury potatoes,
such as King Edward
or Maris Piper, thinly sliced

3 onions, halved and
finely sliced

2 tsp fresh thyme leaves

1 tsp finely chopped fresh
rosemary

00 ml/1 pint chicken stock

salt and pepper

Method

1 Preheat the oven to 160°C/325°F/Gas Mark 3.

2 Trim the chops of any excess fat and place in a
bowl. Add the kidneys to the bowl and season
with salt and pepper to taste.

3 Grease a large, shallow ovenproof dish or deep
roasting tin with half the butter and arrange a
layer of potatoes in the bottom. Layer up the
onions and meat, seasoning with salt and pepper
to taste and sprinkling in the herbs between
each layer. Finish with a neat layer of overlapping
potatoes.

4 Pour in most of the stock so that it covers the
meat. Melt the remaining butter and brush the
top of the potato with it. Reserve any remaining
butter. Cover with foil and cook in the preheated
oven for 2 hours. Uncover the hotpot and brush
the potatoes again with the melted butter. Return
the hotpot to the oven and cook for a further
30 minutes, or until the potatoes are crisp and
brown. Serve immediately.

GRANDMA'S CLASSIC FAVOURITES

PORK & PICKLE PIE

Serves: 10

Prep: 40 mins, plus chilling and cooling

Cook: 1¼ hours

Ingredients

Pastry

450 g/1 lb plain flour, plus extra for dusting

115 g/4 oz butter, chilled and diced, plus extra for greasing

115 g/4 oz white vegetable fat, chilled and diced

7–8 tbsp cold water

salt

milk, to glaze

Filling

800 g/1 lb 12 oz good quality pork sausages, skins removed and roughly chopped

400 g/14 oz pork shoulder, coarsely minced

85 g/3 oz fresh white breadcrumbs

2 tbsp chopped fresh parsley

4 spring onions, trimmed and finely chopped

4 tbsp pickle

salt and pepper

Method

1 To make the pastry, sift the flour and a pinch of salt into a bowl. Add the butter and white vegetable fat and rub in with fingertips until the mixture resembles fine breadcrumbs. Sprinkle over the cold water and mix to a firm dough. Wrap in clingfilm and chill in the refrigerator for 30 minutes.

2 To make the filling, place the sausages, pork shoulder, breadcrumbs, parsley and spring onions in a bowl and mix thoroughly. Season with salt and pepper. Preheat the oven to 200°C/400°F/Gas Mark 6. Grease a 23-cm/9-inch round springform tin.

3 Roll out two thirds of the pastry on a floured surface to a 33-cm/13-inch circle and use to line the prepared tin. Trim the edges. Press half the pork mixture into the pastry case. Spread over the pickle then top with the rest of the pork mixture.

4 Roll out the remaining pastry to a 23-cm/9-inch circle. Brush the rim of the pastry in the tin with water then top with the pastry circle, crimping the edges together firmly to seal. Cut leaves from the pastry trimmings and attach them to the pie with water.

5 Glaze the pie with the milk and pierce two holes in the pastry to allow the steam to escape. Place the tin on a lipped baking sheet. Bake in the preheated oven for 30 minutes, then reduce the oven temperature to 180°C/350°F/Gas Mark 4 and bake for a further 45 minutes. Cool in the tin for 30 minutes, then unclip the tin and leave the pie to cool on the base. Serve warm or cold.

STEAK, ALE & KIDNEY PUDDING

Serves: 4

Prep: 40 mins, plus cooling

Cook: 4½ hours

Ingredients

Filling

600 g/1 lb 5 oz chuck or braising steak, cut into 2.5-cm/1-inch cubes

225 g/8 oz beef or lambs' kidney, trimmed and cut into 1-cm/½ -inch cubes

2 tbsp seasoned flour

25 g/1 oz butter, plus extra for greasing

2–3 tbsp sunflower oil

1 large onion, chopped

225 ml/8 fl oz brown ale

350 ml/12 fl oz beef stock

1 bouquet garni

115 g/4 oz brown cap mushrooms, quartered

Suet pastry

225 g/8 oz self-raising flour, plus extra for dusting

100 g/3½ oz suet

½ tsp salt

1 tsp dried mixed herbs

approx 150 ml/5 fl oz cold water

Method

1 Preheat the oven to 150°C/300°F/Gas Mark 2. Toss the meat in the seasoned flour. Heat the butter and half the oil in a flameproof casserole and fry the meat in batches, until browned. Set aside.

2 Add the remaining oil to the casserole dish and fry the onion for 5 minutes. Stir in the ale and stock and bring to the boil. Return the meat to the pan with the bouquet garni. Cover and cook in the preheated oven for 2 hours. Stir in the mushrooms and leave to cool. Remove the bouquet garni.

3 To make the suet pastry, sift the flour into a large bowl and stir in the suet, salt and dried mixed herbs. Stir in enough of the cold water to make a soft dough. Grease a 1.4-litre/2½ -pint pudding basin.

4 Roll out three quarters of the pastry on a floured surface to a thickness of 15 mm/⅝ inch and use to line the prepared pudding basin, allowing the excess pastry to hang slightly over the edges.

5 Using a slotted spoon, transfer the meat mixture into the basin. Pour in some of the gravy to almost cover the meat (reserve the rest). Roll out the remaining pastry to make a lid. Place the pastry

lid over the filling, brush the pastry edges with water and fold over to seal. Cover with pleated, greased, greaseproof paper and foil and secure with string. Steam the pudding in a covered saucepan half-filled with water for 2½ hours, topping the pan up with boiling water if necessary.

6 Allow to cool slightly, then uncover the pudding and turn out onto a plate. Heat through the reserved gravy to serve with the pudding.

PLOUGHMAN'S LUNCH

Serves: 4

Prep: 20 mins,
plus cooling

Cook: 10–12 mins

Ingredients

4 large eggs

225 g/8 oz British cheese, such as farmhouse Cheddar cheese, Stilton and/or Somerset brie

300 g/10½ oz ready-made pork pie

1 carrot

8 spring onions

16 baby vine tomatoes

4 slices of cured, sliced ham

4 tbsp chutney of your choice

85 g/3 oz salad leaves

crusty bread, to serve

Method

1 First, boil the eggs. Bring a small pan of water to the boil. Gently lower the eggs into the water using a long-handled spoon. Keep the water at a gentle simmer and cook for 6–8 minutes, or until cooked to your liking. Remove the eggs using a slotted spoon and drain quickly on kitchen paper. Leave to cool.

2 When the eggs are cool enough to handle, remove and discard the shells. Cut the eggs in half. Cut the cheese into wedges and the pork pie into quarters. Cut the carrot into batons and trim the spring onions.

3 Arrange all the ingredients on individual serving plates. Serve immediately, accompanied by crusty bread.

FISH & CHIPS WITH MUSHY PEAS

Serves: 4

Prep: 30–35 mins, plus chilling

Cook: 35–40 mins

Ingredients

Batter

225 g/8 oz self-raising flour, plus extra for dusting

½ tsp salt

300 ml/10 fl oz cold lager

Mushy peas

350 g/12 oz frozen peas

30 g/1 oz butter

2 tbsp single cream

salt and pepper

vegetable oil, for deep-frying

6 large floury potatoes, such as King Edward, Maris Piper or Desirée, cut into chips

4 thick cod fillets, about 175 g/6 oz each

salt and pepper

Method

1 Sift the flour into a bowl with the salt and beat or whisk in most of the lager. Check the consistency and add the remaining lager; it should be thick, like double cream. Chill in the refrigerator for half an hour.

2 Cook the peas in lightly salted boiling water for 3 minutes. Drain and mash to a thick purée, add the butter and cream and season with salt and pepper to taste. Set aside and keep warm.

3 Heat the oil to 120°C/250°F in a thermostatically controlled deep fat fryer or a large saucepan using a thermometer. Preheat the oven to 150°C/300°F/Gas Mark 2. Fry the chips for about 8–10 minutes until softened but not coloured. Remove from the oil, drain on kitchen paper and place in a dish in the warm oven. Increase the temperature of the oil to 180°C/350°F.

4 Season the fish with salt and pepper to taste and dust lightly with a little flour. Dip one fillet in the batter and coat thickly. Carefully place in the hot oil and repeat with the other fillets. Cook for 8–10 minutes, turning them over halfway through. Remove the fish from the oil, drain and keep warm.

5 Reheat the oil to 180°C/350°F and recook the chips for a further 2–3 minutes until golden brown. Drain and season with salt and pepper to taste. Serve with the fish and mushy peas.

GRANDMA'S CLASSIC FAVOURITES

VICTORIA SPONGE CAKE

Serves: 8

Prep: 25–30 mins, plus cooling

Cook: 25–30 mins

Ingredients

175 g/6 oz self-raising flour

1 tsp baking powder

175 g/6 oz butter, softened, plus extra for greasing

175 g/6 oz golden caster sugar

3 eggs

icing sugar, for dusting

Filling

3 tbsp raspberry jam

300 ml/10 fl oz double cream, whipped

16 fresh strawberries, halved

Method

1 Preheat the oven to 180°C/350°F/Gas Mark 4. Grease two 20-cm/8-inch sandwich tins and line with baking paper.

2 Sift the flour and baking powder into a bowl and add the butter, sugar and eggs. Mix together, then whisk well until smooth.

3 Divide the mixture evenly between the prepared tins and smooth the surfaces. Bake in the preheated oven for 25–30 minutes, or until well risen and golden brown and the cakes feel springy when lightly pressed.

4 Leave to cool in the tins for 5 minutes, then turn out and peel off the baking paper. Transfer to wire racks to cool completely. Sandwich the cakes together with the raspberry jam, cream and strawberry halves. Dust with icing sugar and serve.

SPOTTED DICK

Serves: 6   **Prep: 20-25 mins**   **Cook: 1-1½ hours**

Ingredients

225 g/8 oz self-raising flour, plus extra for dusting

115 g/4 oz suet

55 g/2 oz caster sugar

150 g/5 oz currants or raisins

grated rind of 1 lemon

150-175 ml/5-6 fl oz milk

2 tsp melted butter, for greasing

ready-made custard, to serve

Method

1 Mix together the flour, suet, sugar, currants and lemon rind in a mixing bowl.

2 Pour in the milk and stir together to give a fairly soft dough.

3 Turn out onto a floured surface and roll into a cylinder. Wrap in greaseproof paper that has been well greased with the melted butter and seal the ends, allowing room for the pudding to rise. Overwrap with foil and place in a steamer over a saucepan of boiling water.

4 Steam for about 1-1½ hours, topping up the water level in the saucepan from time to time.

5 Remove the pudding from the steamer and unwrap. Place on a warmed plate and cut into thick slices. Serve with lots of custard.

GRANDMA'S CLASSIC FAVOURITES

JAM ROLY-POLY

Serves: 6

Prep: 30–25 mins, plus optional resting, plus cooling

Cook: 1½–2 hours

Ingredients

225 g/8 oz self-raising flour

pinch of salt

115 g/4 oz suet

grated rind of 1 lemon

1 tbsp sugar

50 ml/2 fl oz milk, plus 2 tbsp for brushing

50 ml/2 fl oz water

4–6 tbsp strawberry jam

ready-made custard, to serve

Method

1 Sift the flour into a mixing bowl and add the salt and suet. Mix together well. Stir in the lemon rind and the sugar.

2 Mix together the milk and the water in a jug. Make a well in the centre of the dry ingredients and add the liquid ingredients to give a light, elastic dough. Knead lightly until smooth. If you have time, wrap the dough in clingfilm and leave it to rest for 30 minutes.

3 Roll the dough into a 20 x 25-cm/8 x 10-inch rectangle.

4 Spread the jam over the dough, leaving a 1-cm/½-inch border. Brush the border with the milk and roll up the dough carefully, like a Swiss roll, from one short end. Seal the ends. Wrap the roly-poly loosely in greaseproof paper and then in foil, sealing the ends well.

5 Prepare a steamer by half filling it with water and putting it on to boil. Place the roly-poly in the steamer and steam over rapidly boiling water for 1½–2 hours, making sure you top up the water from time to time.

6 When cooked, remove from the steamer and leave to cool slightly. Unwrap, cut into slices and serve immediately with the custard.

GRANDMA'S CLASSIC FAVOURITES

SAUSAGES & MASH WITH ONION GRAVY

Serves: 4 **Prep: 25 mins** **Cook: 1 hour 5 mins**

Ingredients

1 tbsp olive oil

8 good quality sausages

Onion gravy

3 onions, cut in half and thinly sliced

70 g/2½ oz butter

5 ml/4 fl oz Marsala or port

125 ml/4 fl oz vegetable stock

salt and pepper

Mashed potato

900 g/2 lb floury potatoes, such as King Edward, Maris Piper or Desirée, cut into chunks

55 g/2 oz butter

3 tbsp hot milk

tbsp chopped fresh parsley

salt and pepper

Method

1 Place a frying pan over a low heat with the oil and add the sausages. Cover the pan and cook for 25–30 minutes, turning the sausages from time to time, until browned all over.

2 Meanwhile, prepare the onion gravy by placing the onions in a large casserole with the butter and frying over a low heat until soft, stirring continuously. Continue to cook for around 30 minutes, or until the onions are brown and have started to caramelize.

3 Pour in the Marsala and stock and continue to bubble away until the onion gravy is really thick. Season to taste with salt and pepper.

4 To make the mashed potato, cook the potatoes in a large saucepan of lightly salted boiling water for 15–20 minutes. Drain well and mash with a potato masher until smooth. Season with salt and pepper to taste, add the butter, milk and parsley and stir well

5 Serve the sausages immediately with the mashed potato and the onion gravy spooned over the top.

CHICKEN, MUSHROOM & TARRAGON PIE

Serves: 4–6

Prep: 25 mins, plus cooling

Cook: 1 hour 45 mins

Ingredients

1 chicken, about 1.5 kg /3 lb 5 oz

2 fresh tarragon sprigs

1 onion, cut into wedges

300 ml/10 fl oz water

25 g/1 oz butter

175 g/6 oz chestnut mushrooms, sliced

2 tbsp plain flour

55 g/2 oz frozen peas or shelled fresh peas

1 tbsp chopped fresh tarragon

salt and pepper

Pastry

225 g/8 oz plain flour, plus extra for dusting

pinch of salt

175 g/6 oz butter

4 tbsp iced water, plus extra for brushing

1 egg, beaten

Method

1 Preheat the oven to 200°C/400°F/Gas Mark 6.

2 Put the chicken, tarragon sprigs and onion into a casserole dish, add the water and season with salt and pepper. Cover and bake in the preheated oven for 1½ hours. Remove from the oven and lift out the chicken from the casserole dish. Strain the cooking juices into a measuring jug and leave to cool.

3 Meanwhile, make the pastry. Sift the flour with a pinch of salt into a bowl and add the butter and water. Mix to a firm but slightly lumpy dough, adding more iced water if necessary. Roll out into a rectangle on a floured surface, then fold the top third down and the bottom third up. Give the dough a quarter turn, roll out and fold again. Repeat once more, then wrap in clingfilm and chill in the refrigerator.

4 Discard the chicken skin, cut off the meat and dice. Skim off the fat from the cooking juices and make up to 300 ml/10 fl oz with water.

5 Melt the butter in a large saucepan. Cook the mushrooms over a medium heat for 3 minutes. Stir in the flour for 1 minute, then gradually stir in

the cooking juices. Bring to the boil, add the chicken, peas and tarragon and season. Transfer to a pie dish and leave to cool.

Roll out the pastry to 2.5 cm/1 inch larger than the top of the dish. Cut out a 15-mm/⅝-inch strip all the way around. Brush the rim of the dish with water and press the strip onto it. Brush with water and lift the remaining dough on top. Trim off the excess and crimp the edges to seal. Make a slit in the centre and brush with half of the egg. Roll out the trimmings and use to decorate the pie, then brush with the remaining egg. Bake in the preheated oven for 40 minutes until golden. Serve immediately.

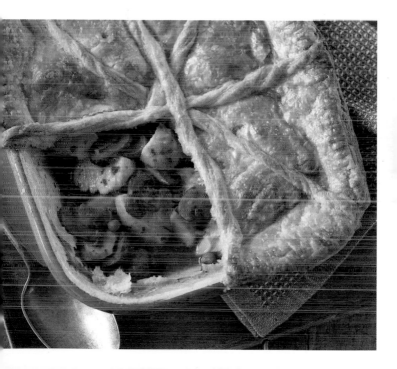

COLCANNON

Serves: 4 **Prep: 25 mins** **Cook: 25–30 mins**

Ingredients

225 g/8 oz green cabbage, shredded

5 tbsp milk

225 g/8 oz floury potatoes, such as King Edward, Maris Piper or Desirée, diced

1 large leek, chopped

pinch of freshly grated nutmeg

knob of butter

salt and pepper

Method

1 Cook the shredded cabbage in a saucepan of boiling salted water for 7–10 minutes. Drain thoroughly and set aside.

2 Meanwhile, in a separate saucepan, bring the milk to the boil and add the potatoes and leek. Reduce the heat and simmer for 15–20 minutes, or until they are cooked through. Remove from the heat, stir in the freshly grated nutmeg and thoroughly mash the potatoes and leek together.

3 Add the drained cabbage to the mashed potato and leek mixture, season to taste and mix together well.

4 Spoon the mixture into a warmed serving dish, making a hollow in the centre with the back of a spoon. Place the butter on top and serve the colcannon at once, while it is still hot.

GAMMON STEAK WITH FRIED EGG & CHIPS

Serves: 4 **Prep: 30 mins** **Cook: 30–35 mins**

Ingredients

vegetable oil, for frying
and brushing

6 large potatoes, such as
Desirée or Maris Piper, cut
into even-sized chips

4 gammon steaks, each
about 175 g/6 oz

4 eggs

salt and pepper

Method

1 Heat enough oil for deep-frying in a large saucepan or deep-fryer to 120°C/250°F, checking the temperature with a thermometer, to blanch the chips. Preheat the oven to 150°C/300°F/Gas Mark 2.

2 Fry the chips for about 8–10 minutes, depending on size, until soft but not coloured. Remove from the oil, drain on kitchen paper and place in a warmed dish in the preheated oven. Increase the temperature of the oil to 180– 90°C/350–375°F, or until a cube of bread browns in 30 seconds.

3 Meanwhile, place the gammon steaks on a grill pan and brush with a little oil. Preheat the grill to high and grill for 3–4 minutes on either side, turning occasionally until the fat is crisp. Set aside and keep warm.

4 Return the chips to the fryer at the increased temperature and cook for a further 2–3 minutes until they are golden brown and crisp. Drain, season well and keep warm. Put 2 tablespoons of oil into a frying pan and heat over a medium heat. Break two eggs into the pan and cook for a few seconds until the white is setting. Tip the pan and spoon the hot oil over the egg yolks so that they become firm but still soft. Remove the eggs from the pan using a wooden spatula and drain on kitchen paper. Keep warm and repeat with the other eggs.

5 Arrange the gammon steaks, egg and chips on warmed plates and serve immediately.

GRANDMA'S CLASSIC FAVOURITES

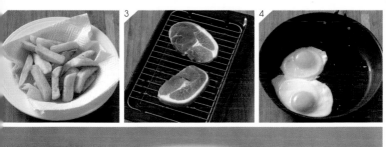

PORK CHOPS WITH APPLE SAUCE

Serves: 4 **Prep: 20–25 mins** **Cook: 30 mins, plus standing**

Ingredients

4 pork rib chops on the bone, each about 3 cm/1¼ inches thick, at room temperature

1½ tbsp sunflower oil or rapeseed oil

salt and pepper

Chunky apple sauce

450 g/1 lb cooking apples, such as Bramley, peeled, cored and diced

4 tbsp caster sugar, plus extra if needed

finely grated zest of ½ lemon

½ tbsp lemon juice, plus extra if needed

4 tbsp water

¼ tsp ground cinnamon

knob of butter

Method

1 Preheat the oven to 200°C/400°F/Gas Mark 6.

2 For the apple sauce, put the apples, sugar, lemon zest, lemon juice and water into a heavy-based saucepan over a high heat and bring to the boil, stirring to dissolve the sugar. Reduce the heat to low, cover and simmer for 15–20 minutes, until the apples are tender and fall apart when you mash them against the side of the pan. Stir in the cinnamon and butter and beat the apples until they are as smooth or chunky as you like. Stir in extra sugar or lemon juice, to taste. Remove the pan from the heat, cover and keep the apple sauce warm.

3 Meanwhile, pat the chops dry and season to taste with salt and pepper. Heat the oil in a large ovenproof frying pan over a medium–high heat. Add the chops and fry for 3 minutes on each side to brown.

4 Transfer the pan to the oven and roast the chops for 7–9 minutes until cooked through and the juices run clear when you cut the chops. Remove the pan from the oven, cover with foil and leave to stand for 3 minutes. Gently reheat the apple sauce, if necessary. Transfer the chops to warmed plates and spoon over the pan juices. Serve immediately, accompanied by the apple sauce.

GRANDMA'S CLASSIC FAVOURITES

APPLE PIE

Serves: 6

Prep: 40–45 mins, plus chilling

Cook: 50 mins

Ingredients

Pastry

350 g/12 oz plain flour, plus extra for dusting

pinch of salt

85 g/3 oz butter or margarine, diced

85 g/3 oz lard or white vegetable fat, diced

6 tbsp cold water

beaten egg or milk, for glazing

Filling

750 g–1 kg/1 lb 10 oz–2 lb 4 oz cooking apples, peeled, cored and sliced

125 g/4½ oz caster sugar, plus extra for sprinkling

½ –1 tsp ground cinnamon, mixed spice or ground ginger

Method

1 To make the pastry, sift the flour and salt into a mixing bowl. Add the butter and lard and rub in with your fingertips until the mixture resembles fine breadcrumbs. Add the water and gather the mixture together into a dough. Wrap the dough in clingfilm and chill in the refrigerator for 30 minutes.

2 Preheat the oven to 220°C/425°F/Gas Mark 7. Roll out almost two thirds of the pastry thinly on a lightly floured surface and use to line a deep 23-cm/9-inch pie dish.

3 To make the filling, place the apple slices, sugar and spice in a bowl and mix together thoroughly. Pack the apple mixture into the pastry case; the filling can come up above the rim. If the apples are not very juicy, add 1–2 tablespoons of water if needed.

4 Roll out the remaining pastry on a lightly floured surface to form a lid. Dampen the edges of the pie rim with water and position the lid, pressing the edges firmly together. Trim the edges. Use the trimmings to cut out leaves to decorate the top of the pie. Dampen and attach. Glaze the top of the pie with beaten egg, make 1–2 slits in the top and place the pie dish on a baking sheet.

5 Bake in the preheated oven for 20 minutes, then reduce the temperature to 180°C/350°F/Gas Mark 4 and bake for a further 30 minutes, or until the pastry is a light golden brown. Serve hot or cold.

GRANDMA'S CLASSIC FAVOURITES

FISHERMAN'S PIE

Serves: 6   **Prep: 35–40 mins**   **Cook: 1 hour**

Ingredients

900 g/2 lb white fish fillets, such as plaice, skinned

150 ml/5 fl oz dry white wine

1 tbsp chopped fresh parsley, tarragon or dill

100 g/3½ oz butter, plus extra for greasing

175 g/6 oz small mushrooms, sliced

175 g/6 oz cooked, peeled prawns

40 g/1½ oz plain flour

125 ml/4 fl oz double cream

900 g/2 lb floury potatoes, such as King Edward, Maris Piper or Desirée, cut into chunks

salt and pepper

Method

1 Preheat the oven to 180°C/350°F/Gas Mark 4. Grease a 1.7-litre/3-pint baking dish. Fold the fish fillets in half and place in the dish. Season well with salt and pepper, pour over the wine and scatter over the herbs. Cover with foil and bake for 15 minutes until the fish starts to flake. Strain off the liquid and reserve for the sauce. Increase the oven temperature to 220°C/425°F/Gas Mark 7.

2 Heat 15 g/½ oz of the butter in a frying pan and sauté the mushrooms. Spoon the mushrooms over the fish and scatter over the prawns. Add 55 g/2 oz of the butter to a saucepan, heat and stir in the flour. Cook for a few minutes without browning, remove from the heat, then add the reserved cooking liquid gradually, stirring well between each addition.

3 Return to the heat and gently bring to the boil, still stirring to ensure a smooth sauce. Add the cream and season to taste with salt and pepper. Pour over the fish in the dish and smooth over the surface.

4 Make the mashed potato by cooking the potatoes in boiling salted water for 15–20 minutes. Drain well and mash with a potato masher until smooth. Season to taste with salt and pepper and add the remaining butter.

5 Pile or pipe the potato onto the fish and sauce and bake in the oven for 10–15 minutes until golden brown

VEGETABLE COBBLER

Serves: 4   **Prep: 35–40 mins**   **Cook: 40 mins**

Ingredients

1 tbsp olive oil

1 garlic clove, crushed

8 small onions, halved

2 celery sticks, sliced

225 g/8 oz swede, chopped

2 carrots, sliced

½ small head of cauliflower, broken into florets

225 g/8 oz button mushrooms, sliced

400 g/14 oz canned chopped tomatoes

55 g/2 oz red lentils, rinsed

2 tbsp cornflour

3–4 tbsp water

300 ml/10 fl oz vegetable stock

2 tsp hot pepper sauce

2 tsp chopped fresh oregano, plus sprigs to garnish

Topping

225 g/8 oz self-raising flour, plus extra for dusting

pinch of salt

4 tbsp butter

115 g/4 oz grated mature Cheddar cheese

2 tsp chopped fresh oregano

1 egg, lightly beaten

150 ml/5 fl oz milk

Method

1 Preheat the oven to 180°C/350°F/Gas Mark 4. Heat the oil in a large frying pan, add the garlic and onions and cook over a low heat for 5 minutes. Add the celery, swede, carrots and cauliflower and cook for 2–3 minutes.

2 Add the mushrooms, tomatoes and lentils. Place the cornflour and water in a bowl and mix to make a smooth paste. Stir into the frying pan with the stock, hot pepper sauce and oregano. Transfer to an ovenproof dish, cover and bake in the preheated oven for 20 minutes.

3 To make the topping, sift the flour and salt together into a bowl. Add the butter and rub it in, then stir in most of the cheese and oregano. Beat the egg with the milk in a small bowl and add enough to the dry ingredients to make a soft dough. Knead, then roll out on a lightly floured work surface to 1 cm/½ inch thick. Cut into 5-cm/2-inch rounds.

4 Remove the dish from the oven and increase the temperature to 200°C/400°F/Gas Mark 6. Arrange the dough rounds around the edge of the dish, brush with the remaining egg and milk mixture and sprinkle with the reserved cheese. Return to the oven and cook for a further 10–12 minutes. Garnish with oregano sprigs and serve.

GRANDMA'S CLASSIC FAVOURITES

ETON MESS

Serves: 6

Prep: 30–35 mins, plus cooling

Cook: 45–50 mins

Ingredients

3 egg whites

175 g/6 oz caster sugar

700 g/1 lb 9 oz strawberries

2 tbsp icing sugar

2 tbsp crème de fraise (strawberry) liqueur (optional)

300 ml/10 fl oz double cream

150 ml/5 fl oz single cream

Method

1 Preheat the oven to 150°C/300°F/Gas Mark 2. Whisk the egg whites in a clean bowl using an electric mixer until thick and in soft peaks. Add the sugar gradually, whisking well after each addition. The meringue mixture should be glossy and firm. Spoon the meringue onto a baking sheet lined with baking paper and spread into a rough 30-cm/12-inch round. Cook in the preheated oven for 45–50 minutes until the meringue is firm on the outside but still soft in the centre. Remove from the oven and allow to cool.

2 Check over the strawberries and hull them. Place a third of the strawberries (choose the larger ones) in a liquidizer and purée with the icing sugar. Pour the purée into a bowl, add the liqueur, if using, and the remaining strawberries and turn in the sauce until well mixed. Whip together the double and single cream until thick but still light and floppy.

3 Break the meringue into large pieces and place half in a large glass serving bowl. Spoon over half the fruit mixture and half the cream. Layer up the remaining ingredients and lightly fold the mixtures together so you have a streaky appearance. Serve immediately after mixing or the meringues will soften.

GRANDMA'S CLASSIC FAVOURITES

RICE PUDDING WITH POACHED RHUBARB

Serves: 12

Prep. 25 mins,
plus cooling

Cook: 1½ hours

Ingredients

butter, for greasing

1.3 litres/2¼ pints whole or
semi-skimmed milk

115 g/4 oz pudding rice

55 g/2 oz caster sugar

1 tsp vanilla extract

freshly grated nutmeg,
for sprinkling

Poached rhubarb

400 g/14 oz rhubarb,
cut into 5-cm/2-inch pieces

100 g/3½ oz caster sugar

3 tbsp water

1–2 tbsp rosewater
or rose syrup

Method

1 Preheat the oven to 160°C/325°F/Gas Mark 3.
Grease a 1.4-litre/ 2½-pint baking dish or pie dish.
Place the milk in a large, heavy-based saucepan
and bring to the boil. Add the rice and boil for
10 minutes, stirring constantly at first so that it
doesn't boil over.

2 Remove from the heat, stir in the sugar and
vanilla extract. Transfer to the prepared dish and
sprinkle with nutmeg. Bake in the preheated
oven for 1¼ hours, or until a brown skin has
formed on top and the pudding is still quite
wobbly underneath.

3 Meanwhile, place the rhubarb in a baking dish or
roasting tin just large enough to hold the pieces
in a single layer. Add the sugar and water, and
then stir the mixture.

4 Cover the tin tightly with foil and bake in the
preheated oven for 30 minutes, or until the
rhubarb is just tender when pierced with the
point of a knife (very thick stems may need a
little longer). Cool for at least 15 minutes, leaving
the foil in place, then gently stir in the rosewater
to taste. Spoon over the rice pudding and serve.

HOME-MADE FISH FINGERS

Serves: 4–6   **Prep: 25 mins**   **Cook: 50–60 mins**

Ingredients

280 g/10 oz thick cod fillets, skin and bones removed

flour, for dusting

1 tsp paprika

fresh breadcrumbs or fine cornmeal, for coating

1 egg, beaten

sunflower oil, for frying

salt and pepper

fresh or frozen peas, cooked, to serve

Sweet potato wedges

450 g/1 lb sweet potatoes, scrubbed and cut into wedges

1 tbsp olive oil

Method

1 To make the potato wedges, preheat the oven to 200°C/400°F/Gas Mark 6. Dry the sweet potato wedges on a clean tea towel. Place the oil in a roasting tin and heat for a few minutes in the oven. Arrange the potatoes in the tin and bake for 30–35 minutes, turning them halfway through, until tender and golden.

2 Meanwhile, cut the cod into strips about 2-cm/¾-inch wide. Put the flour onto a plate, add the paprika and season to taste. Put the breadcrumbs onto a second plate. Roll the cod strips in the seasoned flour until coated, shaking off any excess, then dip them in the beaten egg. Roll the cod strips in the breadcrumbs until evenly coated.

3 Heat enough oil to cover the base of a large, non-stick frying pan. Carefully arrange the fish fingers in the pan – you may have to cook them in batches – and fry them for 3–4 minutes on each side or until crisp and golden. Drain on kitchen paper before serving, if necessary. Serve the fish fingers with the sweet potato wedges and peas.

WINTER VEGETABLE SOUP

Serves: 6   **Prep: 20 mins**   **Cook: 50 mins**

Ingredients

2 tbsp vegetable oil

1 large onion, thickly sliced

1 large potato,
cut into chunks

3 celery sticks, thickly sliced

4 carrots, sliced

175 g/6 oz swede,
cut into chunks

4 large garlic cloves,
peeled and left whole

1.5 litres/2¾ pints chicken
or vegetable stock

225 g/8 oz canned
chopped tomatoes

1 leek, halved lengthways
and thickly sliced

salt and pepper

2 tbsp chopped fresh
flat-leaf parsley, to garnish

grated Cheddar cheese,
to serve

Method

1 Heat the oil in a large, heavy-based saucepan over a medium heat. Add the onion, potato, celery, carrots, swede and garlic cloves. Season to taste with salt and pepper, then cover and cook over a medium heat, stirring occasionally, for 10 minutes.

2 Pour in the stock and tomatoes and bring to the boil. Reduce the heat and simmer, partially covered, for 30 minutes. Add the leek and cook for a further 5 minutes, until just tender.

3 Taste and adjust the seasoning, adding salt and pepper if needed. Ladle into warmed bowls, garnish with the parsley and serve immediately with grated Cheddar cheese.

SUMMER ROAST CHICKEN

Serves: 4

Prep: 30 mins

Cook: 1 hour 35 mins
plus resting

Ingredients

600 g/1 lb 5 oz
new potatoes, scrubbed
and larger ones halved

1 chicken, weighing
1.5 kg/3 lb 5 oz

1 lemon (preferably
unwaxed)

1 tbsp chopped
fresh thyme

2 tbsp olive oil

3 bay leaves

1 garlic bulb,
cloves separated

salt and pepper

green salad, to serve

Method

1 Parboil the potatoes in a pan of lightly salted
   boiling water for 10 minutes, then drain. Preheat
   the oven to 190°C/375°F/Gas Mark 5.

2 Loosen the skin over the chicken breast by
   pushing your fingers underneath, being careful
   not to tear it. Pare the zest from the lemon and
   mix it with the thyme, then push the mixture
   underneath the skin of the chicken. Drizzle in 2
   teaspoons of the oil and season with salt and
   pepper. Cut the lemon in half and push the
   two pieces inside the body cavity with the bay
   leaves, then truss the chicken.

3 Transfer the potatoes to a large roasting tin. Add
   the garlic and remainder of the olive oil and
   toss together. Make a space for the chicken in
   the centre of the roasting tin and roast in the
   preheated oven for 1 hour 25 minutes, stirring
   and turning the potatoes once or twice during
   cooking. To check the chicken is cooked
   through, pierce the thickest part of the thigh
   with a skewer – when the juices run clear, it is
   ready. Cover and rest the chicken for 10–15
   minutes before carving. Serve with the roast new
   potatoes and green salad.

CARAMELIZED ONION TART

Serves: 4–6

Prep: 25 mins plus resting

Cook: 50–55 mins

Ingredients

100 g/3½ oz unsalted butter

600 g/1 lb 5 oz onions, thinly sliced

2 eggs

100 ml/3½ fl oz double cream

100 g/3½ oz Gruyère cheese, grated

20-cm/8-inch ready-baked pastry case

100 g/3½ oz coarsely grated Parmesan-style cheese

salt and pepper

Method

1 Melt the butter in a heavy-based frying pan over a medium heat. Add the onions and cook, stirring frequently to avoid burning, for 30 minutes, or until well-browned and caramelized. Remove the onions from the pan and set aside.

2 Preheat the oven to 190°C/375°F/Gas Mark 5. Beat the eggs in a large bowl. Stir in the cream and season to taste with salt and pepper. Add the Gruyère cheese and mix well. Stir in the cooked onions.

3 Pour the egg and onion mixture into the baked pastry case and sprinkle with the Parmesan-style cheese.

4 Place on a baking sheet and bake in the preheated oven for 15–20 minutes, until the filling has set and is beginning to brown. Remove from the oven and leave to rest for at least 10 minutes.

5 Cut the tart into slices and serve hot or at room temperature.

★ Variation

For a delicious accompanying salad, toss together rocket leaves with halved cherry tomatoes and add 4 tablespoons of parmesan cheese and 2 tablespoons of olive oil. Season to taste.

HOME COMFORTS

LUXURY CAULIFLOWER CHEESE

Serves: 4   **Prep: 25 mins**   **Cook: 30–40 mins**

Ingredients

600 g/1 lb 5 oz cauliflower florets (1 medium cauliflower)

150 ml/5 fl oz dry white wine

1 bay leaf

450 ml/16 fl oz milk

25 g/1 oz butter, cut into pieces

25 g/1 oz plain flour

70 g/2½ oz mature Cheddar cheese, grated

40 g/1½ oz Parmesan cheese, grated

1 tsp English mustard

1 tbsp snipped fresh chives

1 tbsp chopped fresh parsley

salt

Method

1 Cook the cauliflower in a large saucepan of lightly salted boiling water for 6–8 minutes until tender but still firm to the bite. Drain well. Preheat the oven to 200°C/400°F/Gas Mark 6. Alternatively, preheat the grill to high.

2 Place the wine and bay leaf in a saucepan. Boil rapidly until the wine is reduced by half. Add the milk, butter and flour and whisk with a hand whisk until the butter has melted. Continue whisking until the sauce boils and thickens. Simmer for 1 minute.

3 Remove from the heat. Mix the cheeses together and stir two thirds into the sauce until smooth, then stir in the mustard, chives and parsley. Remove the bay leaf from the sauce.

4 Spoon a little of the sauce over the base of a shallow baking dish. Tip the cauliflower into the dish and spread out in an even layer. Spoon the remaining sauce over the top and sprinkle with the rest of the cheese. Bake in the preheated oven for 20 minutes until lightly browned and bubbling. Alternatively brown under the grill. Serve hot.

★ Variation

For an extra delicious dish cut some cooked bacon into strips or lardons and sprinkle over the top.

LEEK & POTATO SOUP

Serves: 4–6　　　**Prep: 20–25 mins**　　　**Cook: 30 mins**

Ingredients

55 g/2 oz butter

1 onion, chopped

3 leeks, sliced

225 g/8 oz potatoes, cut into 2-cm/¾-inch cubes

850 ml/1½ pints vegetable stock

salt and pepper

150 ml/5 fl oz single cream (optional), to serve

2 tbsp snipped fresh chives, to garnish

Method

1　Melt the butter in a large saucepan over a medium heat, add the prepared vegetables and sauté gently for 2–3 minutes, until soft but not brown. Pour in the stock and bring to the boil then reduce the heat and simmer, covered, for 15 minutes.

2　Remove from the heat and liquidize the soup in the saucepan using a hand-held stick blender if you have one. Alternatively, pour into a blender, liquidize until smooth and return to the rinsed-out saucepan.

3　Reheat the soup and season to taste with salt and pepper. Ladle into warmed bowls and serve swirled with the cream, if using, and garnished with the chives.

CREAM OF TOMATO SOUP

Serves: 6   **Prep: 25 mins**   **Cook: 30–40 mins**

Ingredients

25 g/1 oz butter

1 tbsp olive oil

1 onion, finely chopped

1 garlic clove, chopped

900 g/2 lb plum tomatoes, chopped

700 ml/1¼ pints vegetable stock

125 ml/4 fl oz dry white wine

2 tbsp sun-dried tomato purée

2 tbsp torn fresh basil leaves, plus extra leaves to garnish

150 ml/5 fl oz double cream

salt and pepper

Method

1 Melt the butter with the oil in a large, heavy-based saucepan. Add the onion and cook, stirring occasionally, for 5 minutes, or until softened. Add the garlic, tomatoes, stock, wine and tomato purée, stir well and season to taste. Partially cover the saucepan and simmer, stirring occasionally, for 20–25 minutes, or until the mixture is soft and pulpy.

2 Remove the saucepan from the heat, leave to cool slightly, then pour into a blender or food processor. Add the torn basil and process. Push the mixture through a sieve into a clean saucepan with a wooden spoon.

3 Stir in the cream and reheat the soup, but do not let it boil. Ladle the soup into warmed bowls, garnish with the basil leaves and serve immediately.

QUICHE LORRAINE

Serves: 4

Prep: 30–35 mins, plus cooling

Cook: 50 mins

Ingredients

4 eggs

175 g/6 oz cooked ham

3 spring onions, finely chopped

150 ml/5 fl oz milk, plus extra to glaze

salt and pepper

Pastry

250 g/9 oz plain flour

115 g/4 oz butter

pinch of salt

2–3 tbsp cold water, to mix

Method

1 Preheat the oven to 200°C/400°F/Gas Mark 6.

2 To make the pastry, put the flour into a bowl, rub in the butter until the mixture resembles fine breadcrumbs, then add the salt and enough water to make a smooth dough.

3 Bring a saucepan of water to the boil. Gently lower 2 of the eggs into the water using a long-handled spoon. Keep the water at a gentle simmer and cook for 8 minutes. Remove the eggs and cool under cold running water.

4 Divide the pastry in two, one piece slightly large than the other, and roll out the larger piece to line a 20-cm/8-inch flan tin.

5 Peel the hard-boiled eggs carefully and wipe to make sure there are no pieces of shell attached to the eggs. Chop the eggs and cut the ham into small pieces. Place the eggs, ham and onions in the pastry case.

6 Beat the remaining eggs with the milk, season well with salt and pepper and pour over the ham mixture.

Roll out the other piece of pastry, dampen the edge of the pastry base and lay the lid on top. Seal well and crimp the edges of the quiche. Glaze with a little milk and place the quiche on a baking sheet.

Bake in the preheated oven for 10 minutes then reduce the oven temperature to 180°C/350°F/Gas Mark 4 and bake for a further 30 minutes, until the pastry is golden. Serve warm or cold.

IRISH RAREBIT

Serves: 4　　　　**Prep: 20 mins**　　　　**Cook: 5 mins**

Ingredients

225 g/8 oz mild Cheddar cheese, roughly grated

25 g/1 oz lightly salted butter

4 tbsp full fat milk

1 tsp cider vinegar

1 tsp mustard powder

4 slices wholemeal or soda bread

2 tbsp chopped dill pickles

salt and pepper

Method

1 Preheat the grill until hot. Put the cheese, butter and milk in a saucepan and heat gently, stirring until creamy and smooth. Add the vinegar, mustard and seasoning to the sauce.

2 Toast the bread on one side only. Place on a baking tray, uncooked side facing upwards. Pour the sauce over the bread. Place under the preheated grill for 2–3 minutes, until golden and bubbling.

3 Sprinkle with the chopped pickles and serve immediately.

BAKED EGGS WITH CREAM, SPINACH & PARMESAN

Serves: 2   **Prep: 20 mins**   **Cook: 12 mins**

Ingredients

2 tbsp butter, plus extra
for greasing

125 g/4½ oz baby spinach

½ tsp freshly grated nutmeg

4 small eggs

4 tbsp single cream

2 tbsp freshly grated
Parmesan cheese

salt and pepper

Method

1 Preheat the oven to 160°C/325°F/Gas Mark 3.
   Lightly grease 2 individual ceramic gratin dishes
   or similar.

2 Melt the butter in a large frying pan over low
   heat and add the spinach. Cook for 1 minute,
   stirring with a wooden spoon until the spinach
   starts to wilt. Season with a little nutmeg, then
   divide between the prepared dishes.

3 Gently break 2 eggs into each dish. Pour the
   cream over them and sprinkle with grated
   Parmesan, then season with salt and pepper.
   Bake in the preheated oven for 10 minutes, or
   until the whites of the eggs have set but the yolks
   remain runny. Serve at once.

BACON & POTATO CAKES

Serves: 4   **Prep: 30 mins**   **Cook: 35–40 mins**

Ingredients

550 g/1 lb 4 oz floury
potatoes, cut into
even-sized chunks

8 rindless bacon rashers

1 tbsp lightly salted butter

½ tsp sea salt flakes

½ tsp black pepper

2 tbsp snipped chives

4 tbsp fine oatmeal

1 egg, lightly beaten

plain flour, for dusting

rapeseed oil or vegetable
oil, for frying

watercress sprigs, to garnish

Method

1 Add the potatoes to a large saucepan of salted boiling water, cover, bring back to the boil and simmer gently for 20 minutes, until tender. Drain well and put back in the pan. Cover with a clean kitchen cloth for a few minutes to get rid of excess moisture.

2 While the potatoes are cooking, cook the bacon over a medium-high heat for 5–6 minutes, until crisp. Drain on kitchen paper. Set aside 4 rashers and keep warm. Chop the remaining rashers finely.

3 Mash the potatoes with the butter, sea salt and pepper until creamy. Stir in the chopped bacon, chives, oatmeal and beaten egg.

4 With floured hands, form the potato mixture into four flat cakes about 7 cm/2¾ inches in diameter.

5 Heat about 1 cm/½ inch of oil in a heavy-based saucepan over a medium heat. Add the potato cakes and cook for about 4 minutes on each side, until golden brown.

6 Transfer the potato cakes to warmed serving plates. Top with the watercress and reserved bacon rashers, and serve immediately.

HOME COMFORTS

BEEF & STOUT PIES

Makes: 4

Prep: 35–40 mins
plus cooling

Cook: 2 hours 20 mins

Ingredients

3 tbsp plain flour

1 tsp salt

½ tsp black pepper

900 g/2 lb boneless
braising beef, cut into
2.5-cm/1-inch pieces

vegetable oil, for frying

300 ml/10 fl oz meat stock

1 onion, roughly chopped

225 g/8 oz chestnut
mushrooms, stalks
discarded, caps quartered

1 tbsp tomato purée

2 tsp chopped fresh thyme

250 ml/9 fl oz stout

450 g/1 lb ready-made
puff pastry

1 egg yolk, lightly beaten

Method

1 Combine the flour, salt and pepper in a bowl, then toss the beef in the mixture until evenly coated.

2 Heat 3 tablespoons of oil in a large frying pan over a medium–high heat. Brown the beef, in batches, and transfer to a flameproof casserole. Deglaze the frying pan with 4 tablespoons of stock, and add the liquid to the casserole.

3 Heat another 1–2 tablespoons of oil in the frying pan and cook the onion and mushroom for 6–7 minutes, until soft. Add to the casserole with the tomato purée, thyme, stout and remaining stock. Heat the casserole over a medium–high heat, bring to the boil, then simmer gently with the lid slightly askew for 1½ hours. Check the seasoning.

4 Drain the meat mixture in a sieve set over a bowl, reserving the liquid. Leave until cool. Preheat the oven to 220°C/425°F/Gas Mark 7. Put a baking tray in the oven to heat.

5 Divide the meat mixture among four individual 400-ml/14-fl oz pie dishes with a flat rim or ovenproof bowls. Pour in enough of the liquid to not quite cover the filling. Dampen the rims of the pie dishes

6 Cut the pastry into quarters. Roll out each piece to about 2.5 cm/1 inch bigger than the dishes. Cut a 1-cm/½-inch strip from each quarter and press it onto a dampened rim. Brush with egg yolk, then drape the pastry quarter on top, covering the strip. Trim, crimp the edges with a fork and make three slashes down the middle. Decorate the tops with shapes cut from the trimmings. Brush with the remaining egg yolk.

7 Place the pies on the preheated baking tray and bake in the preheated oven for 20 minutes. Reduce the heat to 200°C/400°F/Gas Mark 6 and bake for a further 5 minutes until golden.

SWEET POTATO, SWEDE & MUSHROOM HASH

Serves: 4   **Prep: 20–25 mins**   **Cook: 25–30 mins**

Ingredients

3 tbsp olive oil

500 g/1 lb 2 oz sweet potatoes, diced

280 g/10 oz swedes, diced

1 onion, chopped

175 g/6 oz streaky bacon, sliced, or lardons

250 g/9 oz mushrooms, sliced

4 eggs

salt and pepper

chopped fresh, flat leaf parsley to garnish

Method

1 Heat the oil in a large, lidded frying pan over a high heat. Add the sweet potatoes and swedes, stir in the oil to coat and season to taste with salt and pepper. Cook, stirring occasionally for 10–15 minutes, or until the vegetables are just turning golden and soft.

2 Add the onion and bacon, stir well and continue to cook for 5 minutes until the onion is soft and the bacon is cooked. Stir in the mushrooms, cover the pan and cook for a further 5 minutes.

3 Make four indentations in the mixture and carefully break an egg into each one. Cover the pan and cook for a further 3–4 minutes, or until the egg whites are firm but the yolks are still soft. Garnish with parsley and serve immediately.

GAMMON STEAKS WITH PARSLEY SAUCE

Serves: 4 **Prep: 20 mins** **Cook: 30–40 mins**

Ingredients

4 unsmoked gammon steaks, 2 cm/¾ inch thick, about 200 g/7 oz each

vegetable oil, for brushing

Parsley sauce

25 g/1 oz unsalted butter

1 shallot, finely chopped

3 tbsp plain flour

175 ml/6 fl oz ham or chicken stock

250 ml/9 fl oz full fat milk

5 tbsp chopped fresh parsley

squeeze of lemon juice

½ tsp mustard powder

salt and white pepper

Method

1 First make the parsley sauce. Melt the butter in a frying pan over a medium–low heat. Add the shallo and cook for 2–3 minutes, until soft but not coloured

2 Remove the frying pan from the heat and stir in the flour. Return to the heat and cook for 1 minute, stirring. Reduce the heat to low, and whisk in the stock and milk. Keep whisking until the sauce starts to bubble. Stir in the parsley, then add the lemon juice, mustard, pepper and a pinch of salt. Simmer gently, stirring often, for 20 minutes.

3 Meanwhile, remove the rind but not the fat from the gammon steaks. Slash the fat at 2-cm/¾-inch intervals. Brush with oil on both sides.

4 Heat a ridged griddle pan over a high heat. Cook the steaks on one side for 5–6 minutes. Once they start to colour on the underside, cove with a lid and reduce the heat to medium. Turn and cook the other side for 5 minutes, covered.

5 Place the steaks on warmed serving plates, pour the sauce over them and serve.

QUICK SPAGHETTI BOLOGNESE

Serves: 4   **Prep: 20 mins**   **Cook: 35 mins**

Ingredients

2 tbsp olive oil

1 large onion, chopped

500 g/1 lb 2 oz lean beef mince

1 green pepper, deseeded and chopped

1 garlic clove, crushed

150 ml/5 fl oz red wine or beef stock

400 g/14 oz canned chopped plum tomatoes

2 tbsp tomato purée

1 tbsp dried oregano

200 g/7 oz dried spaghetti

salt and pepper

freshly grated Parmesan cheese, to serve

Method

1 Heat the oil in a large saucepan over a high heat.

2 Add the onion and mince and fry, stirring until lightly browned with no remaining traces of pink.

3 Stir in the green pepper and garlic. Add the wine, tomatoes, tomato purée and oregano. Bring to the boil and boil rapidly for 2 minutes.

4 Reduce the heat, cover and simmer for 20 minutes, stirring occasionally.

5 Meanwhile, bring a large saucepan of lightly salted water to the boil, add the spaghetti, bring back to the boil and cook for about 8–10 minutes, until tender but still firm to the bite.

6 Drain the spaghetti in a colander and return to the pan.

7 Season the sauce to taste with salt and pepper, then stir into the spaghetti.

8 Serve immediately, with Parmesan cheese.

SAUSAGE ROLLS

Makes: 8

Prep: 25–30 mins, plus cooling

Cook: 30–35 mins

Ingredients

2 tsp sunflower oil

1 small onion, finely chopped

2 tsp chopped fresh sage

450 g/1 lb pork sausage meat

2 tsp wholegrain mustard

25 g/1 oz fresh white breadcrumbs

350 g/12 oz ready-rolled puff pastry

salt and pepper

1 egg beaten with 1 tbsp water, to glaze

Method

1 Heat the oil in a frying pan and gently fry the chopped onion for 8–10 minutes until soft and pale golden. Transfer to a large bowl, stir in the chopped sage and leave to cool. Preheat the oven to 200°C/400°F/Gas Mark 6.

2 Add the sausage meat to the bowl with the mustard and breadcrumbs. Season with salt and pepper and mix thoroughly with a fork. Unroll the pastry sheet and cut in half lengthways. Divide the sausage meat mixture into two equal portions and lay along the length of each strip of pastry in a cylinder shape.

3 Brush one long edge of each strip of pastry with some of the egg and water mixture and fold over the pastry to enclose the filling. Press the edges together well to seal and cut each roll into four shorter lengths. Lightly dampen a large baking sheet with cold water and place the sausage rolls on it, spaced well apart. Glaze the pastry with the egg and water mixture. Bake in the preheated oven for 20–25 minutes until crisp and golden. Transfer to a wire rack and serve warm or cold.

HOME COMFORTS

POTATO PANCAKES

Serves: 6   **Prep: 25 mins**   **Cook: 11–17 mins**

Ingredients

4 large potatoes, coarsely grated

1 large onion, grated

2 eggs, lightly beaten

5 g/2 oz fine matzo meal

1 tsp salt

pepper

sunflower oil, for frying

To serve

soured cream

ly sliced smoked salmon

snipped chives

Method

1 Preheat the oven to 110°C/225°F/Gas Mark ¼ and line a heatproof plate with kitchen paper. Working in small batches, put the potatoes on a tea towel, fold over the tea towel and squeeze to extract as much water as possible.

2 Put the potatoes in a large bowl, add the onion, eggs, matzo meal and the salt. Add pepper to taste and mix together.

3 Heat a large, heavy-based frying pan over a medium-high heat. Add a thin layer of oil and heat until hot. Drop 2 tablespoons of the mixture into the pan and flatten slightly. Add as many more pancakes as will fit without overcrowding the pan. Fry for 2 minutes, or until crisp and golden underneath. Flip or turn with a palette knife and continue frying for a further 1–2 minutes, until crisp and golden.

4 Repeat using the remaining batter. Meanwhile, transfer the cooked pancakes to the prepared plate and keep warm in the oven. Add extra oil to the pan between batches, if necessary. Serve the pancakes hot, topped with soured cream and salmon and sprinkled with chives.

HOME COMFORTS

SPAGHETTI ALLA CARBONARA

Serves: 4 **Prep: 20 mins** **Cook: 15 mins**

Ingredients

450 g/1 lb dried spaghetti

1 tbsp olive oil

225 g/8 oz rindless pancetta or streaky bacon, chopped

4 eggs

5 tbsp single cream

2 tbsp freshly grated Parmesan cheese

salt and pepper

Method

1 Bring a large, heavy-based saucepan of lightly salted water to the boil, add the pasta, bring back to the boil and cook for 8–10 minutes, or until tender but still firm to the bite.

2 Meanwhile, heat the oil in a heavy-based frying pan. Add the pancetta and cook over a mediu heat, stirring frequently, for 8–10 minutes.

3 Beat the eggs with the cream in a small bowl and season to taste with salt and pepper. Drain the pasta and return it to the saucepan. Tip in the contents of the frying pan, then add the eg mixture and half the cheese. Stir well, then transf the spaghetti to a warmed serving dish. Serve immediately, sprinkled with the remaining chees

KIPPER & POTATO SALAD
WITH MUSTARD DRESSING

Serves: 4-6   Prep: 25-30 mins   Cook: 15-20 mins

Ingredients

50 g/1 lb 7 oz waxy new potatoes, scrubbed

tbsp chopped fresh dill, plus sprigs to garnish

ring onions, some green ps included, diagonally sliced

dishes, sliced into rounds

4 kipper fillets, about 70 g/2½ oz each

salt and pepper

Mustard dressing

spoon mustard powder

pinch of sugar

2 tbsp cider vinegar

2 tbsp double cream

3 tbsp groundnut oil

3 tbsp olive oil

salt and pepper

Method

1 Cook the potatoes in boiling salted water for 15–20 minutes, or until just tender. Drain and slice widthways into 5-mm/¼-inch pieces. Set aside to cool.

2 To make the dressing, combine the mustard, sugar, salt and pepper, cider vinegar and double cream. Gradually add the oils, whisking until smooth and thick.

3 Put the potatoes in a bowl, and mix with the dressing and dill. Add most of the spring onions and radishes, reserving a few to garnish. Check the seasoning, and add more salt and pepper if necessary.

4 Remove the skin from the kipper fillets. Slice each fillet lengthways into four, then slice each piece widthways into thin bite-sized strips.

5 Divide the potato mixture among individual serving plates. Arrange the kipper strips attractively on top, and garnish with the reserved spring onions, radishes and dill sprigs.

BACON BUTTIES WITH HOME-MADE TOMATO SAUCE

Serves: 2

Prep: 25–30 mins, plus cooling and storing

Cook: 35 mins

Ingredients

Tomato sauce (makes about 250 ml/ 9 fl oz)

2 tbsp olive oil

1 red onion, chopped

2 garlic cloves, chopped

250 g/9 oz plum tomatoes, chopped

250 g/9 oz canned chopped tomatoes

½ tsp ground ginger

½ tsp chilli powder

40 g/1½ oz dark brown sugar

100 ml/3½ fl oz red wine vinegar

salt and pepper

4 rashers smoked bacon

30 g/1 oz butter, softened

4 slices thick brown or white bread

pepper

Method

1 To make the tomato sauce, heat the olive oil in a large saucepan and add the onion, garlic and tomatoes. Add the ginger and chilli and season with salt and pepper to taste. Cook for 15 minutes, or until soft.

2 Pour the mixture into a food processor and blend well. Sieve thoroughly to remove all the seeds. Return the mixture to the pan and add the sugar and vinegar. Return to the boil and cook until it is the consistency of ketchup.

3 Bottle quickly in sterilized bottles or jars and store in a cool place or refrigerator until ready to serve.

4 Place the rashers of bacon under a hot grill and grill, turning frequently until the bacon is crisp and golden brown. Spread the butter over the slices of bread.

5 Place two rashers on the base pieces of bread, season with pepper to taste and spoon the sauce over the bacon. Top with the other slice of bread and serve immediately.

EGG & BACON PIE

Serves: 4–6

Prep: 25–30 mins, plus chilling and cooling

Cook: 50–55 mins

Ingredients

Pastry

100 g/3½ oz salted butter

200 g/7 oz plain flour, plus extra for dusting

1–2 tbsp cold water

Filling

15 g/½ oz butter

1 small onion, finely chopped

4 lean streaky bacon rashers, diced

55 g/2 oz Cheddar cheese, grated

2 eggs, beaten

300 ml/10 fl oz single cream

pepper

Method

1 For the pastry, rub the butter into the flour with your fingertips until the mixture resembles fine breadcrumbs. Stir in just enough water to bind the mixture to a firm dough. Roll out on a lightly floured surface and use to line a 23-cm/9-inch loose-based round tart tin. Prick the base all over with a fork. Chill for at least 10 minutes.

2 Preheat the oven to 200°C/400°F/Gas Mark 6. Line the pastry case with baking paper and beans, place on a baking tray and bake for 10 minutes. Remove the paper and beans and bake for a further 10 minutes.

3 For the filling, melt the butter in a frying pan and cook the onion and bacon for about 5 minutes until the onion is softened and lightly browned. Spread the mixture in the pastry case and sprinkle with half the cheese. Beat together the eggs and cream and season with pepper. Pour into the pastry case and sprinkle with the remaining cheese.

4 Reduce the oven temperature to 190°C/375°F/Gas Mark 5. Bake the pie for 25–30 minutes, or until golden brown and just set. Cool for 10 minutes before turning out.

BEEF BURGERS

Makes: 4 **Prep: 20 mins** **Cook: 20 mins**

Ingredients

650 g/1 lb 7 oz fresh
beef mince

1 red pepper, deseeded
and finely chopped

1 garlic clove,
finely chopped

2 small red chillies,
deseeded and
finely chopped

1 tbsp chopped fresh basil

½ tsp ground cumin

salt and pepper

fresh basil sprigs, to garnish

burger buns, to serve

Method

1 Preheat the grill to medium–high. Put the beef,
   red pepper, garlic, chillies, chopped basil and
   cumin into a bowl.

2 Mix until well combined and season to taste
   with salt and pepper.

3 Using your hands, form the mixture into
   four burger shapes. Place the burgers under the
   preheated grill and cook for 5–8 minutes.

4 Using a spatula or fish slice, turn the burgers
   and cook on the other side for 5–8 minutes. To
   check the burgers are cooked through, cut into
   the middle to check that the meat is no longer
   pink. Any juices that run out should be clear and
   piping hot with visible steam rising.

5 Garnish with basil sprigs and serve immediately in
   burger buns.

EGGY BREAD

Serves: 2   **Prep: 15 mins**   **Cook: 5 mins**

Ingredients

1 large egg

4 tbsp milk or single cream

2 slices day-old
thick white bread

30 g/1 oz butter

Method

1 Break the egg into a shallow bowl and whisk well.
Stir in the milk.

2 Dip the bread into the egg mixture and coat
both sides well.

3 Heat half of the butter in a frying pan over a
medium heat and gently fry one piece of eggy
bread for about 1 minute on each side, or until
golden brown and crispy. Take care not to let it
burn. Remove from the pan and keep warm. Melt
the remaining butter and repeat with the other
piece of bread. Serve immediately.

MEATBALLS

Serves: 4

Prep: 30 mins,
plus cooling

Cook: 35 mins

Ingredients

1 tbsp olive oil

1 small onion,
finely chopped

2 garlic cloves,
finely chopped

2 fresh thyme sprigs,
finely chopped

650 g/1 lb 7 oz
fresh beef mince

25 g/1 oz fresh
breadcrumbs

1 egg, lightly beaten

salt and pepper

Sauce

1 onion, cut into wedges

3 red peppers,
halved and deseeded

400 g/14 oz canned
chopped tomatoes

1 bay leaf

Method

1 Heat the oil in a frying pan. Add the onion and
garlic and cook over a low heat for 5 minutes,
or until soft. Place in a bowl with the thyme, beef
mince, breadcrumbs and egg. Season to taste with
salt and pepper, mix thoroughly and shape into 20
golf-ball sized balls.

2 Heat a large frying pan over a low–medium heat.
Add the meatballs and cook, stirring gently for 15
minutes. To check that the meat is cooked through
cut into the middle to check that there are no
remaining traces of pink.

3 Meanwhile, to make the sauce, preheat the grill. Cook
the onion wedges and red pepper halves under a
preheated grill, turning frequently, for 10 minutes, until
the pepper skins are blistered and charred.

4 Put the peppers into a polythene bag, tie the top
and leave to cool. Set the onion wedges aside. Peel
off the pepper skins and roughly chop the flesh.
Put the pepper flesh into a food processor with the
onion wedges and tomatoes. Process to a smooth
purée and season to taste with salt and pepper.

5 Pour into a saucepan with the bay leaf and bring
to the boil. Reduce the heat and simmer, stirring
occasionally, for 10 minutes. Remove and discard
the bay leaf. Serve the sauce immediately with
the meatballs.

FRIED CHICKEN WINGS

Serves: 4   **Prep: 25 mins**   **Cook: 25 mins**

Ingredients

12 chicken wings
1 egg
4 tbsp milk
70 g/2½ oz plain flour
1 tsp paprika
225 g/8 oz breadcrumbs
55 g/2 oz butter
salt and pepper

Method

1 Preheat the oven to 220°C/425°F/Gas Mark 7.
Separate each chicken wing into three pieces,
discarding the bony tip. Beat the egg with the
milk in a shallow dish.

2 Combine the flour, paprika, and salt and pepper
to taste in a shallow dish. Place the breadcrumb
in another dish. Dip the chicken in the egg
mixture, drain and roll in the flour.

3 Shake off any excess, then roll the chicken
wings in the breadcrumbs, gently pressing then
onto the surface and shaking off any excess.

4 Put the butter in a wide, shallow roasting tin and
place in the preheated oven to melt.

5 Place the chicken in the tin skin side down.

6 Bake for 10 minutes on each side. To check that
the wings are cooked through, cut into the midc
to check that there are no remaining traces of
pink or red. Any juices that run out should be cle
and piping hot with visible steam rising.

7 Transfer the chicken to a serving platter and serv

BEEF IN STOUT WITH HERB DUMPLINGS

Serves: 6   **Prep: 35 mins**   **Cook: 2 hours 40 mins**

Ingredients

Stew

2 tbsp sunflower oil

2 large onions, thinly sliced

8 carrots, sliced

4 tbsp plain flour

1.25 kg/2 lb 12 oz stewing steak, cut into cubes

425 ml/15 fl oz stout

2 tsp muscovado sugar

2 bay leaves

1 tbsp chopped fresh thyme

salt and pepper

Herb Dumplings

115 g/4 oz self-raising flour

pinch of salt

55 g/2 oz shredded suet

2 tbsp chopped fresh parsley, plus extra to garnish

about 4 tbsp water

Method

1 Preheat the oven to 160°C/325°F/Gas Mark 3. Heat the oil in a flameproof casserole. Add the onions and carrots and cook over a low heat, stirring occasionally, for 5 minutes, or until the onions are softened. Meanwhile, place the flour in a polythene bag and season well with salt and pepper. Add the stewing steak to the bag, tie the top and shake well to coat. Do this in batches, if necessary. Reserve any remaining seasoned flour.

2 Remove the onions and carrots from the casserole with a slotted spoon and reserve. Add the stewing steak to the casserole, in batches, and cook, stirring frequently, until browned all over. Return all the meat and the onions and carrots to the casserole and sprinkle in the reserved seasoned flour. Pour in the stout and add the sugar, bay leaves and thyme. Bring to the boil, cover and cook in the preheated oven for 1¾ hours.

3 To make the herb dumplings, sift the flour and salt into a bowl. Stir in the suet and parsley and add enough of the water to make a soft dough. Shape into small balls between the palms of your hands. Add to the casserole and return to the oven for 30 minutes. Remove and discard the bay leaves. Serve immediately, sprinkled with parsley.

BOILED EGGS WITH SOLDIERS

Serves: 2   **Prep: 15 mins**   **Cook: 10 mins**

Ingredients

4 large eggs
salt and pepper

Soldiers

crusty white loaf,
sliced and cut into
thick fingers, buttered

Method

1 Bring a small pan of water to the boil – it is useful to use a small pan to prevent the eggs rolling around too freely and cracking. The water should be deep enough to cover the eggs.

2 Gently lower the eggs into the water using a long-handled spoon. Keep the water at a gentle simmer and cook for 3–4 minutes for a runny yolk and set white, or 4–5 minutes for a firmer egg.

3 Remove the eggs from the pan using a slotted spoon, drain quickly on kitchen paper and place in egg cups.

4 Season with salt and pepper to taste and serve immediately with the soldiers.

SMOKED COD CHOWDER

Serves: 4   **Prep: 20 mins**   **Cook: 35 mins**

Ingredients

25 g/1 oz butter

1 onion, finely chopped

1 small celery stick, finely diced

250 g/9 oz potatoes, diced

55 g/2 oz carrots, diced

300 ml/10 fl oz boiling water

350 g/12 oz smoked cod fillets, skinned and cut into bite-sized pieces

300 ml/10 fl oz milk

salt and pepper

fresh flat-leaf parsley sprigs, to garnish

Method

1 Melt the butter in a large saucepan over a low heat, add the onion and celery and cook, stirring frequently, for 5 minutes, or until soft but not brown.

2 Add the potatoes, carrots, water and salt and pepper to taste. Bring to the boil, then reduce the heat and simmer for 10 minutes, or until the vegetables are tender. Add the fish to the chowder and cook for a further 10 minutes.

3 Pour in the milk and heat gently. Taste and adjust the seasoning, adding salt and pepper if necessary. Ladle into warmed bowls and serve, garnished with parsley sprigs.

STEAK & ENGLISH MUSTARD SANDWICH

Serves: 2

Prep: 20–25 mins

Cook: 25–30 mins,
plus resting

Ingredients

15 g/½ oz butter

2 tbsp olive oil

1 onion, halved
and thinly sliced

½ tsp brown sugar

2 rump steaks, each
about 175 g/6 oz weight
and 2 cm/¾ inch thick

1 tsp coarsely ground
black pepper

4 tbsp mayonnaise

2 tsp ready-made
English mustard

4 thick slices crusty
white bread

25 g/1 oz rocket leaves

salt and pepper

Method

1 Heat the butter and half the oil in a frying pan
and fry the sliced onion gently for 10 minutes
until softened. Season with salt and pepper and
sprinkle over the sugar. Increase the heat a little
and continue cooking for a further 5 minutes until
golden and caramelized.

2 Heat a cast-iron griddle pan until very hot. Drizzle
the remaining oil over the steaks, coat with the
black pepper and season lightly with salt. Add
the steaks to the pan and cook over a high heat
for 3–5 minutes on each side, until cooked to your
liking. Remove the steaks from the pan, cover
and leave to rest in a warm place for 10 minutes.

3 Mix together the mayonnaise and mustard
and spread thickly over two slices of the bread.
Top with the rocket leaves. Using a sharp knife,
thinly slice the steaks on an angle. Pile the steak
on top of the rocket leaves and top with the
caramelized onions. Sandwich with the remaining
slices of bread and serve immediately.

MUSHROOM & ONION QUICHE

Serves: 4

Prep: 25 mins, plus chilling and cooling

Cook: 1 hour 20 mins

Ingredients

butter, for greasing

200 g/7 oz shortcrust pastry

flour, for dusting

Filling

55 g/2 oz unsalted butter

3 red onions, halved and sliced

350 g/12 oz mixed wild mushrooms, such as ceps, chanterelles and morels

2 tsp chopped fresh thyme

1 egg

2 egg yolks

100 ml/3½ fl oz double cream

salt and pepper

Method

1 Preheat the oven to 190°C/375°F/Gas Mark 5. Lightly grease a 23-cm/9-inch loose-based quiche tin. Roll out the dough on a lightly floured work surface and use to line the tin. Line the pastry case with baking paper and fill with baking beans. Chill in the refrigerator for 30 minutes. Bake in the preheated oven for 25 minutes. Remove the paper and beans and cool on a wire rack. Reduce the oven temperature to 180°C/350°F/Gas Mark 4.

2 To make the filling, melt the butter in a large, heavy-based frying pan over a very low heat. Add the onions, cover and cook, stirring occasionally, for 20 minutes. Add the mushrooms and thyme and cook, stirring occasionally, for a further 10 minutes. Spoon into the pastry case and put the tin on a baking sheet.

3 Lightly beat the egg, egg yolks, cream and salt and pepper to taste in a bowl. Pour over the mushroom mixture. Bake in the oven for 20 minutes, or until the filling is set and golden. Serve hot or at room temperature.

BUBBLE & SQUEAK

Serves: 4   **Prep: 30 mins**   **Cook: 40–45 mins**

Ingredients

450 g/1 lb floury potatoes,
such as King Edward,
Maris Piper or Desirée,
cut into chunks

55 g/2 oz butter

3 tbsp hot milk

450 g/1 lb green cabbage

4 tbsp olive oil

1 onion, thinly sliced

salt and pepper

Method

1 Bring a large saucepan of lightly salted water to
the boil, add the potatoes and cook for 15–20
minutes. Drain well and mash with a potato
masher until smooth. Season with salt and pepper,
add the butter and milk and stir well.

2 Cut the cabbage into quarters, remove the stalk
and finely shred the leaves.

3 Heat half of the oil in a large frying pan, add the
onion and fry until soft. Add the cabbage to the
pan and stir-fry for 2–3 minutes until soft. Season
with salt and pepper, add the potato and mix
together well.

4 Press the mixture firmly into the frying pan and
leave to cook over a high heat for 4–5 minutes
until the base is crispy. Place a plate over the pan
and invert the pan so that the potato cake falls
onto the plate. Add the remaining oil to the pan,
reheat, and slip the cake back into the pan with
the uncooked side down.

5 Continue to cook for a further 5 minutes until the
base is crispy. Turn out onto a warmed plate, cut
into wedges and serve immediately.

POT ROAST

Serves: 6   **Prep: 30–35 mins**   **Cook: 3 hours 40 mins**

Ingredients

4–5 potatoes, cut into large chunks

2½ tbsp plain flour

1 rolled brisket joint, weighing 1.6 kg/3 lb 8 oz

2 tbsp vegetable oil

2 tbsp butter

1 onion, finely chopped

2 celery sticks, diced

2 carrots, peeled and diced

1 tsp dill seed

1 tsp dried thyme

350 ml/12 fl oz red wine

150–225 ml/5–8 fl oz beef stock

salt and pepper

2 tbsp chopped fresh dill, to serve

Method

1 Bring a large saucepan of lightly salted water to the boil. Add the potatoes, bring back to the boil and cook for 10 minutes. Drain and set aside. Preheat the oven to 140°C/275°F/Gas Mark 1. Mix 2 tablespoons of the flour with 1 teaspoon salt and ¼ teaspoon pepper in a large shallow dish. Dip the meat in the flour to coat.

2 Heat the oil in a flameproof casserole, add the meat and brown. Transfer to a plate. Add half the butter to the casserole, then add the onion, celery, carrots, dill seed and thyme and cook for 5 minutes. Return the meat and juices to the casserole. Pour in the wine and enough stock to reach one third of the way up the meat, and bring to the boil. Cover and cook in the oven for 3 hours, turning the meat every 30 minutes. Add the potatoes and more stock, if necessary, after 2 hours.

3 When ready, transfer the meat and vegetables to a warmed serving dish. Strain the cooking liquid to remove any solids, then return the liquid to the casserole. Mix the remaining butter and flour to a paste. Bring the cooking liquid to the boil. Whisk in small pieces of the flour and butter paste, whisking constantly until the sauce is smooth. Pour the sauce over the meat and vegetables. Sprinkle with fresh dill and serve.

★ Variation

For a spicer dish add ¼ teaspoon of ground allspice along with the herbs in step 2, for a heartier pot roast.

HOME COMFORTS

FAMILY CELEBRATION DINNERS

ROAST TURKEY

Serves: 8

Prep: 20–25 mins

Cook: 3½ hours,
plus resting

Ingredients

115 g/4 oz ready-made
sausage stuffing

1 turkey, weighing 5 kg/11 lb

40 g/1½ oz butter

bay leaves, sage leaves
and chives, to garnish

To serve

ready-made bread sauce

roast potatoes

roast vegetables

Method

1 Preheat the oven to 220°C/425°F/Gas Mark 7.
Prepare the stuffing and spoon it into the neck
cavity of the turkey and close the flap of skin
with a skewer. Place the bird in a large roasting
tin and rub it all over with the butter. Roast in the
preheated oven for 1 hour, then lower the oven
temperature to 180°C/350°F/Gas Mark 4 and
roast for a further 2½ hours. You may need to
pour off the fat from the roasting tin occasionally.

2 Check that the turkey is cooked by inserting
a skewer or the point of a sharp knife into the
thickest part of the thigh – if the juices run clear,
it is ready. Transfer the bird to a carving board,
cover loosely with foil and leave to rest.

3 Garnish the turkey with bay and sage leaves
and chives. Carve and serve roughly 150 g/5½
oz of turkey per person, with the warm bread
sauce, roast potatoes and vegetables.

★ Variation

Sausage meat pairs well with many festive
flavours. Try adding a pinch of nutmeg, some
grated apple or even chopped cranberries
before cooking.

FAMILY CELEBRATION DINNERS

GLAZED GAMMON IN CIDER

Serves: 6–8

Prep: 30 mins, plus cooling

Cook: 4½ hours

Ingredients

4 kg/9 lb gammon
1 apple, cored and chopped
1 onion, chopped
300 ml/10 fl oz cider
6 black peppercorns
1 bouquet garni
1 bay leaf
about 50 cloves
4 tbsp demerara sugar

Method

1 Put the gammon in a large saucepan and add enough cold water to cover. Bring to the boil and skim off any foam that rises to the surface. Reduce the heat and simmer for 30 minutes.

2 Drain the gammon and return to the saucepan. Add the apple, onion, cider, peppercorns, bouquet garni, bay leaf and a few of the cloves. Pour in enough fresh water to cover and bring back to the boil. Cover and simmer for 3 hours 20 minutes.

3 Preheat the oven to 200°C/400°F/Gas Mark 6. Take the saucepan off the heat and set aside to cool slightly. Remove the gammon from the cooking liquid and, while it is still warm, loosen the rind with a sharp knife, then peel it off and discard.

4 Score the fat into diamond shapes and stud with the remaining cloves. Place the gammon on a rack in a roasting tin and sprinkle with the sugar. Roast in the preheated oven, basting occasionally with the cooking liquid, for 20 minutes. To check it is cooked, insert a skewer into the centre of the meat – the juices should run clear. Serve hot or cold.

POACHED SALMON

Serves: 6

Prep: 25–30 mins,
plus cooling/standing

Cook: 12–18 mins

Ingredients

1 whole salmon (head on),
about 2.7 kg/6 lb to 3.6 kg/
8 lb prepared weight

3 tbsp salt

3 bay leaves

10 black peppercorns

1 onion, sliced

1 lemon, sliced

lemon wedges, to serve

Method

1 Wipe the salmon thoroughly inside and out with kitchen paper, then use the back of a cook's knife to remove any scales that might still be on the skin. Remove the fins with scissors and trim the tail. Some prefer to cut off the head but it is traditionally prepared with it on.

2 Place the salmon on the two-handled rack that comes with a fish kettle, then place it in the kettle. Fill the kettle with enough cold water to cover the salmon adequately. Sprinkle over the salt, bay leaves and peppercorns and scatter in the onion and lemon slices.

3 Place the kettle over a low heat, over two burners, and bring just to the boil very slowly. Cover and simmer very gently. To serve cold, simmer for 2 minutes only, remove from the heat and leave to cool in the liquor for about 2 hours with the lid on. To serve hot, simmer for 6–8 minutes and leave to stand in the hot water for 15 minutes before removing. Remove the fish from the kettle, skin and serve with lemon wedges for squeezing over.

MUSHROOM STROGANOFF

Serves: 4   **Prep: 15–20 mins**   **Cook: 15–20 mins**

Ingredients

25 g/1 oz butter

1 onion, finely chopped

450 g/1 lb closed-cup mushrooms, quartered

1 tsp tomato purée

1 tsp wholegrain mustard

150 ml/5 fl oz crème fraîche

1 tsp paprika, plus extra to garnish

salt and pepper

fresh flat-leaf parsley sprigs, to garnish

Method

1 Heat the butter in a large, heavy-based frying pan. Add the onion and cook gently for 5–10 minutes until soft.

2 Add the mushrooms to the frying pan and stir-fry for a few minutes until they begin to soften.

3 Stir in the tomato purée and mustard, then add the crème fraîche. Cook gently, stirring constantly for 5 minutes.

4 Stir in the paprika and season to taste with salt and pepper.

5 Garnish with extra paprika and parsley sprigs and serve immediately.

BEEF WELLINGTON

Serves: 6

Prep: 35 mins,
plus cooling and chilling

Cook: 1 hour–1 hour
20 mins

Ingredients

2 tbsp olive or vegetable oil

1.5 kg/3 lb 5 oz beef fillet,
cut from the middle
of the fillet, trimmed
of fat and sinew

55 g/2 oz butter

150 g/5½ oz mushrooms,
chopped

2 garlic cloves, crushed

150 g/5½ oz
smooth liver pâté

few drops of truffle oil
(optional)

1 tbsp finely chopped fresh
parsley

2 tsp English mustard

500 g/1 lb 2 oz puff pastry

1 egg, lightly beaten

salt and pepper

roasted root vegetables,
to serve

Method

1 Place a large frying pan over a high heat and add the
olive oil. Rub salt and pepper to taste into the beef and
sear very quickly all over in the pan. (This method gives a
rare version. If you want it less rare, roast it at 220°C/425°F/
Gas Mark 7 for 20 minutes at this stage.) Set aside to cool.

2 Heat the butter in a frying pan over a medium heat, add
the mushrooms and fry for 5 minutes. Reduce the heat,
add the garlic and fry for another 5 minutes. Put the
mushrooms and garlic in a bowl, add the pâté, truffle oil
if using, and parsley, and beat with a fork. Leave to cool.

3 Rub the mustard into the seared beef fillet. Roll out the
pastry into a rectangle large enough to wrap the whole
fillet with some to spare. Spread the mushroom paste
in the middle of the pastry, leaving a 5-cm/2-inch gap
between the paste and the edge of the pastry, and
lay the beef on top. Brush the edges of the pastry with
beaten egg and fold it over, edges overlapping, and
across the meat to completely enclose it.

4 Preheat the oven to 220°C/425°F/Gas Mark 7. Place
the wrapped beef in a roasting tin with the join
underneath and brush with beaten egg. Leave to
chill in the refrigerator for 15 minutes, then transfer
to the preheated oven and bake for 50 minutes.
Check after 30 minutes – if the pastry looks golden
brown, cover with foil to prevent it burning. Serve
immediately with roasted root vegetables.

PRAWN COCKTAIL WITH QUAIL EGGS

Serves: 4

Prep: 25 mins, plus cooling

Cook: 10 mins

Ingredients

8 quail eggs

6 tbsp mayonnaise

3 tbsp Greek-style yogurt

2 tbsp tomato ketchup

dash of hot pepper sauce

2 tsp lime juice

40 g/1½ oz peppery salad leaves

5-cm/2-inch piece of cucumber, finely diced

1 small ripe avocado, peeled and thinly sliced

225 g/8 oz cooked king prawns, peeled and tails left intact

salt and pepper

lime wedges and fresh dill sprigs, to garnish

Method

1 Bring a small saucepan of water to the boil then reduce to a simmer. Gently lower the quail eggs into the water and simmer for 5 minutes. Drain and cool under running cold water. Once cold, shell and set aside.

2 Place the mayonnaise, yogurt, ketchup, hot pepper sauce and lime juice in a bowl and mix together thoroughly. Season to taste with salt and pepper.

3 Divide the salad leaves between four large wine or cocktail glasses. Scatter over the diced cucumber. Halve the eggs and arrange on top of the salad with the avocado slices and prawns (reserving eight prawns to garnish).

4 Spoon over the mayonnaise dressing. Serve garnished with the reserved prawns, lime wedges and sprigs of dill.

FAMILY CELEBRATION DINNERS

POTTED CRAB

Serves: 4

Prep: 25 mins,
plus cooling and chilling

Cook: 2-3 mins

Ingredients

140 g/5 oz cooked white
crabmeat

85 g/3 oz cooked brown
crabmeat

¼ tsp cayenne pepper

2 tbsp lemon juice

150 g/5½ oz butter,
softened

salt and pepper

fresh parsley sprigs,
to garnish

lemon wedges
and Melba toast
or crusty bread, to serve

Method

1 Place the white and brown crabmeat in a bowl and mix together with a fork. Stir in the cayenne pepper and lemon juice and season with salt and pepper.

2 Add 85 g/3 oz of the butter and beat until thoroughly combined. Divide the mixture between four 125-ml/4-fl oz ramekin dishes and level the surface.

3 Place the remaining butter in a small saucepan and heat gently until melted. Cool for 5 minutes then skim off any white froth with a spoon. Pour the melted butter in a thin stream over the top of each pot of crab mixture to cover evenly, leaving any sediment in the base of the pan. Leave until cold then place the ramekins in the refrigerator for about 2 hours until the butter is firm.

4 Remove the ramekins from the refrigerator about 30 minutes before serving. Garnish with parsley sprigs and serve with lemon wedges and Melba toast or crusty bread.

SEA TROUT WITH CIDER & CREAM SAUCE

Serves: 8–10   **Prep: 35 mins**   **Cook: 1½ hours**

Ingredients

oil, for brushing

1 whole sea trout or salmon, gutted, weighing about 3.5 kg/7 lb 10 oz

small bunch parsley, plus a few extra sprigs to garnish

2 fresh bay leaves

sea salt flakes

black pepper

1 leek, halved lengthways and sliced

2 lemons, thinly sliced

50 g/1¾ oz lightly salted butter

250 ml/9 fl oz dry cider

250 ml/9 fl oz single cream

3 tbsp chopped fresh tarragon or dill

boiled new potatoes and freshly cooked peas, to serve

Method

1 Preheat the oven to 180°C/350°F/Gas Mark 4. Line a roasting tin with thick foil large enough to loosely enclose the fish in a sealed parcel. Brush the inside of the foil with oil. Remove the head, tail and fins from the fish. Place the fish on the foil and stuff the cavity with the parsley and bay leaves. Rub all over with sea salt flakes and black pepper. Arrange the leek slices and half the lemon slices over the fish, and dot with the butter. Gather up the foil and pour the cider around the fish. Seal the foil well, leaving a small vent at the top.

2 Place the fish parcel in its roasting tin in the preheated oven and bake for 1¼ hours, or until the thickest part of the flesh looks opaque when pierced with the tip of a knife. Open the foil and carefully slide the fish onto a warm serving platter, discarding the parsley, bay leaves, lemon and leek. Keep warm.

3 Transfer the juices from the foil into the pan, along with any that flow from the fish, and place on the hob over a medium–high heat. Stir in the cream and tarragon, then simmer briskly for 10–15 minutes until slightly thickened. Check the seasoning and pour into a jug.

4 Remove the skin from the top of the fish. Garnish with the remaining lemon slices and parsley sprigs. Serve with the sauce, new potatoes and peas.

FAMILY CELEBRATION DINNERS

PORK FILLET WITH ROASTED RHUBARB

Serves: 4

Prep: 30 mins

Cook: 55–60 mins, plus resting

Ingredients

800 g/1 lb 12 oz boneless pork loin

olive oil

1 tsp sea salt flakes

½ tsp black pepper

10 small sprigs of rosemary

125 ml/4 fl oz chicken stock

175 g/6 oz pink rhubarb stalks, trimmed and sliced diagonally into 4-cm/1½-inch lengths

1 tbsp honey

Method

1 Preheat the oven to 190°C/375°F/Gas Mark 5. Using the tip of a sharp knife, score the fat, but not the flesh, of the pork at 1-cm/½-inch intervals. Tie the meat with kitchen twine to form a neat roll. You can ask your butcher to do both of these.

2 Place the meat in a small roasting tin. Rub with oil and then with the sea salt and black pepper, rubbing them in well. Insert the rosemary sprigs into the slits in the fat. Roast in the preheated oven for 40 minutes.

3 Pour in the stock. Arrange the rhubarb around the meat and drizzle with the honey. Roast for another 10–15 minutes, until the rhubarb is tender and starting to colour at the edges.

4 Transfer the pork and rhubarb to a warmed serving platter, reserving the pan juices. Make a tent over the meat with foil and leave to rest for 10 minutes in a warm place.

5 Place the roasting tin on the hob over a medium-high heat. Let bubble rapidly to reduce the pan juices, including any that have flowed from the meat, for 3–4 minutes, until slightly thickened. Check the seasoning, strain into a jug and serve with the meat.

ROAST GOOSE WITH APPLE STUFFING & CIDER GRAVY

Serves: 4–5

Prep: 45–55 mins, plus drying and cooling

Cook: 5¼ hours, plus resting

Ingredients

1 goose, weight about 4 kg/9 lb, with the giblets (the neck, heart and gizzard) and lumps of fat in the cavity reserved, and wing tips and leg tips cut off and reserved

1 onion, roughly chopped

1 celery stick, roughly chopped

1 large carrot, roughly chopped

handful of parsley

2–3 thyme sprigs

2 fresh bay leaves

½ tsp black peppercorns

2 small firm apples

250 ml/9 fl oz dry cider

2 tbsp apple cider vinegar

2 tbsp plain flour

salt and pepper

Method

1 Prick the goose all over with a fork and place in a colander. Douse with lots of boiling water, then pat dry with kitchen paper. Season inside the cavity with salt and pepper, and rub salt all over the skin. Leave to dry.

2 To make the stuffing, heat a knob of the goose fat in a frying pan over a medium heat, add the onion and cook until soft. Add the bacon, potatoes, apples, sage, thyme, salt and pepper. Gently cook, covered, for 20 minutes until the apples are soft. Add the liver, parsley and lemon zest, and cook for 5 minutes. Spread out the stuffing in a wide bowl and leave to cool.

3 Meanwhile, make a stock. Put the reserved wing and leg tips and giblets in a saucepan. Add the vegetables, herbs and peppercorns. Pour in enough cold water to just cover. Slowly bring to the boil, covered, reduce the heat and simmer with the lid askew for 2 hours.

4 Preheat the oven to 200°C/400°F/Gas Mark 6. Spoon the stuffing into the goose cavity. Insert an apple at each end to hold the stuffing in place and seal the flaps with cocktail sticks. Truss the wings and legs with twine. Put the goose in a roasting tin and cook for 30 minutes, then pour

Apple stuffing

3 onions, chopped

4 unsmoked streaky bacon rashers, chopped

500 g/1 lb 2 oz floury potatoes, cut into 1-cm/½-inch dice

3 cooking apples, quartered, cored, peeled and roughly chopped

1½ tbsp chopped fresh sage

1 tbsp chopped fresh thyme

½ tsp sea salt

¼ tsp black pepper

115 g/4 oz goose liver, chopped

2 tbsp chopped fresh parsley

finely grated zest of 1 lemon

the fat. Reduce the temperature to 180°C/350°F/ Gas Mark 4. Cover the goose loosely with foil and cook for 1½ hours, pouring off the fat twice more at 30-minute intervals. Add some water if the tin looks dry. Remove the foil and roast for 30 minutes, until the juices run clear when the thickest part of the thigh is pierced with a skewer. Lift the goose on to a warmed platter, cover with foil and leave to rest for 20 minutes.

5 To make the gravy, strain 500 ml/17 fl oz of stock and blot up any fat that rises. Pour off the fat from the roasting tin. Stir in the cider and vinegar, heat over a medium heat, scraping up any sediment in the pan. Add the flour and stir for a minute, until blended. Pour in the strained stock. Bring to the boil, simmer for 5 minutes and strain.

6 Slice the apples and arrange around the goose. Carve the goose and serve with the sliced apples, stuffing and cider gravy.

PRIME RIB OF BEEF AU JUS

Serves: 8

Prep: 20–25 mins, plus standing

Cook: 1 hour 55 mins–2½ hours, plus resting

Ingredients

2.7 kg/6 lb rib of beef

55 g/2 oz butter, softened

1½ tsp sea salt flakes

1 tbsp ground black pepper

2 tbsp flour

1 litre/1¾ pints beef stock

thyme sprigs, to garnish

roast potatoes and freshly cooked vegetables, to serve

Method

1 Place the beef bone-side down in a deep-sided flameproof roasting tin. Rub the entire surface of the meat with butter, and coat evenly with the salt and black pepper.

2 Leave the beef to reach room temperature for 1 hour. Preheat the oven to 230°C/450°F/Gas Mark 8. Place the meat in the preheated oven and allow to roast uncovered for 20 minutes to sear the outside of the roast.

3 Reduce the heat to 160°C/325°F/Gas Mark 3 and roast for 15 minutes per 450 g/1 lb of meat for medium-rare (plus or minus 15 minutes for well done and rare respectively). Transfer the meat to a large platter and cover with foil. Allow to rest for 30 minutes before serving.

4 Pour off all but 2 tablespoons of the fat from the pan and place the roasting tin over a medium heat. Add the flour to the roasting pan and simmer, stirring with a wooden spoon for 1 minute to form a thick paste. Pour in a ladleful of beef stock, bring to the boil, stirring and scraping all the caramelized beef drippings from the bottom of the pan. Repeat with the remaining stock, a ladleful at a time. Simmer for 10 minutes.

5 Serve the beef with the 'jus' accompanied by roast potatoes and vegetables and garnished with thyme.

CHICKEN LIVER PÂTÉ

Serves: 6

Prep: 25 mins, plus cooling and chilling

Cook: 15 mins

Ingredients

200 g/7 oz butter

225 g/8 oz trimmed chicken livers, thawed if frozen

2 tbsp Marsala wine or brandy

1½ tsp chopped fresh sage

1 garlic clove, roughly chopped

150 ml/5 fl oz double cream

salt and pepper

fresh bay leaves or sage leaves, to garnish

Melba toast, to serve

Method

1 Melt 40 g/1½ oz of the butter in a large, heavy-based frying pan. Add the chicken livers and cook over a medium heat for 4 minutes on each side. They should be brown on the outside but still pink in the centre. Transfer to a food processor and process until finely chopped.

2 Stir the Marsala into the frying pan, scraping up any sediment with a wooden spoon, then add to the food processor with the chopped sage, garlic and 100 g/3½ oz of the remaining butter. Process until smooth. Add the cream, season to taste and process until thoroughly combined and smooth. Spoon the pâté into a dish or individual ramekins, smooth the surface and leave to cool completely.

3 Melt the remaining butter in a small saucepan, allow to cool for 5 minutes, skim off any white froth then spoon over the surface of the pâté, leaving any sediment in the saucepan. Garnish with herb leaves, leave to cool, then cover and chill in the refrigerator. Serve with Melba toast.

FAMILY CELEBRATION DINNERS

GLAZED BEETROOT & EGG SOURDOUGH TOASTS

Serves: 2–4   **Prep: 25 mins**   **Cook: 12–15 mins**

Ingredients

4 eggs

500 g/1 lb 2 oz cooked beetroot (fresh or vacuum-packed without vinegar)

2 tsp sugar, or to taste

5 tsp cider vinegar, or to taste

4 slices sourdough bread

6 tbsp olive oil

1 tbsp Dijon mustard

3 tbsp chopped fresh dill

salt and pepper

Method

1 Cook the eggs in a pan of boiling water for 8 minutes, then drain, shell and chop them. Set aside. Dice the beetroot quite small and place in a small bowl. Mix in half the sugar and 1 teaspoon of the vinegar and season to taste with salt and pepper.

2 Preheat the grill to medium–high. Brush the bread with a little of the oil and toast under the preheated grill for 2–3 minutes, until crisp and golden.

3 Meanwhile, drizzle 1 teaspoon of the remaining oil over the beetroot. Whisk together the remaining vinegar and sugar with the mustard and salt and pepper to taste. Gradually whisk in the remaining oil to make a thick dressing. Stir in the dill and taste for seasoning – it should be sweet and mustardy, with a sharpness – add more sugar or vinegar if you wish.

4 Turn the bread over and top with the beetroot, giving it a stir first, covering the slices right up to the crusts. Glaze the beetroot under the grill for 2–3 minutes, until browned in places.

5 Cut the slices in half or quarters and top with the reserved chopped egg. Drizzle with a little dressing and serve immediately.

FAMILY CELEBRATION DINNERS

GARLIC & HERB DUBLIN BAY PRAWNS

Serves: 2   **Prep: 25 mins,**   **Cook: 5–6 mins**
                     plus marinating

Ingredients

12 raw Dublin Bay prawns
in their shells

juice of ½ lemon

2 garlic cloves, crushed

3 tbsp chopped
fresh parsley

1 tbsp chopped fresh dill

3 tbsp softened butter

salt and pepper

lemon wedges
and crusty bread,
to serve

Method

1 Rinse the prawns. Devein, using a sharp knife to
   slice along the back from the head end to the
   tail and removing the thin black intestine.

2 Mix the lemon juice with the garlic, herbs and
   butter to form a paste. Season well with salt and
   pepper. Spread the paste over the prawns and
   leave to marinate for 30 minutes. Meanwhile,
   preheat the grill to medium.

3 Cook the prawns under the preheated grill for
   5–6 minutes. Alternatively, heat a frying pan
   and fry the prawns until cooked. Turn out onto
   warmed plates and pour over the pan juices.
   Serve immediately with lemon wedges and
   crusty bread.

FAMILY CELEBRATION DINNERS

DEVILS & ANGELS ON HORSEBACK

Makes: 32   **Prep: 25–30 mins**   **Cook: 10–15 mins**

Ingredients

Devils

8 rindless lean bacon rashers

8 canned anchovy fillets in oil, drained

16 whole blanched almonds

16 ready-to-eat prunes

Angels

8 rindless lean bacon rashers

16 smoked oysters, drained if canned

sprigs of fresh thyme, to garnish

Method

1 Preheat the oven to 200°C/400°F/Gas Mark 6.

2 For the devils, cut each bacon rasher lengthways in half and gently stretch with the back of a knife. Cut each anchovy fillet lengthways in half. Wrap half an anchovy around each almond and press them into the cavity where the stones have been removed from the prunes. Wrap a strip of bacon around each prune and secure with a cocktail stick.

3 For the angels, cut each bacon rasher lengthways in half and gently stretch with the back of a knife. Wrap a bacon strip around each oyster and secure with a cocktail stick.

4 Put the devils and angels onto a baking sheet and cook in the preheated oven for 10–15 minutes until sizzling hot and the bacon is cooked. Garnish with sprigs of fresh thyme and serve hot.

FAMILY CELEBRATION DINNERS

LASAGNE

Serves: 4   **Prep: 25–30 mins**   **Cook: 1 hour 25 mins**

Ingredients

2 tbsp olive oil

55 g/2 oz pancetta, chopped

1 onion, chopped

1 garlic clove, finely chopped

225 g/8 oz fresh beef mince

2 celery sticks, chopped

2 carrots, chopped

pinch of sugar

½ tsp dried oregano

400 g/14 oz canned chopped tomatoes

2 tsp Dijon mustard

450 ml/16 fl oz ready-made cheese sauce

225 g/8 oz dried no pre-cook lasagne sheets

115 g/4 oz freshly grated Parmesan cheese, plus extra for sprinkling

salt and pepper

Method

1 Preheat the oven to 190°C/375°F/Gas Mark 5. Heat the oil in a large, heavy-based saucepan. Add the pancetta and cook over a medium heat, stirring occasionally, for 3 minutes.

2 Add the onion and garlic and cook, stirring occasionally, for 5 minutes, or until soft.

3 Add the beef mince and cook, breaking it up with a wooden spoon, until brown all over with no remaining traces of pink. Stir in the celery and carrots and cook for 5 minutes

4 Season to taste with salt and pepper. Add the sugar, oregano and tomatoes and their can juices. Bring to the boil, reduce the heat and simmer for 30 minutes.

5 Meanwhile, stir the mustard into the cheese sauce. In a large, rectangular ovenproof dish, make alternate layers of meat sauce, lasagne sheets and Parmesan cheese.

6 Pour the cheese sauce over the layers, covering them completely, and sprinkle with Parmesan cheese. Bake in the preheated oven for 30 minutes, or until golden brown and bubbling. Serve immediately.

FAMILY CELEBRATION DINNERS

CROWN OF ROAST LAMB

Serves: 6

Prep: 30 mins,
plus cooling

Cook: 2¼ hours–2 hours
35 mins, plus resting

Ingredients

1.6 kg/3 lb 8 oz
crown of lamb

2 tbsp olive oil

salt and pepper

Stuffing

100 g/3½ oz
long-grain rice

2 tbsp vegetable oil

1 onion, finely chopped

2 celery sticks,
finely chopped

2 garlic cloves, crushed

25 g/1 oz shelled pistachios

zest of 1 lemon,
juice of ½ lemon

2 tbsp finely chopped mint

2 tbsp finely chopped
parsley

100 g/3½ oz raisins

Method

1 Calculate the cooking time of the lamb by
allowing 25 minutes per 450 g/1 lb plus 25 minutes
for medium, or 30 minutes per 450 g/1 lb plus 30
minutes for well done. Place the crown in a deep
roasting tin, brush the outside with the oil and
season with salt and pepper. Preheat the oven to
180°C/350°F/Gas Mark 4.

2 To make the stuffing, cook the rice until just al
dente. Drain and cool. Heat the oil in a frying pan
and sauté the onion and celery for 4–5 minutes.
Add the garlic and cook for a further 1 minute
until softened but not browned. Stir into the
cooled rice, together with the pistachios, lemon
zest and juice, herbs and raisins.

3 Fill the centre of the crown with the stuffing,
cover the ends of the bones with foil to prevent
burning, then cover the whole joint with foil. Roast
for the calculated time, removing the foil for the
last 10–15 minutes. At the end of the cooking
time, remove from the oven, lift out of the tin, re-
cover completely with foil and allow to rest for 20
minutes. Serve with the stuffing.

GAME PIE

Serves: 6

Prep: 35 mins, plus cooling

Cook: 2 hours–2 hours 25 mins

Ingredients

2 tbsp sunflower oil

800 g/1 lb 12 oz boneless mixed game (such as venison, rabbit and pheasant), cut into 2.5-cm/1-inch cubes

225 g/8 oz shallots, halved

1 garlic clove, chopped

100 g/3½ oz smoked bacon lardons

175 g/6 oz carrots, chopped

2 tbsp flour, plus extra for dusting

300 ml/10 fl oz chicken stock

200 ml/7 fl oz red wine

2 tbsp redcurrant jelly

few sprigs of fresh thyme

500 g/1 lb 2 oz puff pastry

salt and pepper

beaten egg, to glaze

Method

1 Heat half of the oil in a large flameproof casserole dish. Fry the game meat in batches until brown, then remove with a slotted spoon and set aside. Add the rest of the oil to the dish and fry the shallots, garlic, bacon and carrots for 10 minutes, stirring, until browned.

2 Add the flour to the dish and cook for one minute then stir in the stock, red wine and redcurrant jelly and bring to the boil. Return the game meat to the dish with the thyme sprigs. Season with salt and pepper then cover and simmer very gently for 1–1¼ hours, or until the meat is tender. Leave to cool for 1 hour.

3 Preheat the oven to 220°C/425°F/Gas Mark 7. Transfer the game casserole to a large oval pie dish and place a pie funnel in the centre of the dish. Dampen the rim of the dish with cold water.

4 Roll out the pastry on a lightly floured surface to an oval at least 5 cm/2 inches wider all round than the dish. Cut a 2.5-cm/1-inch strip of pastry from the outer edge, brush with water and use to line the rim of the dish. Brush the pastry rim with water and top with the oval pastry lid. Seal, trim and crimp the pastry edges and decorate the top of the pie with pastry trimmings.

5 Glaze the pie with the beaten egg. Bake in the preheated oven for 30–35 minutes until the pastry is risen and golden. Serve immediately.

FAMILY CELEBRATION DINNERS

PUMPKIN & CHESTNUT RISOTTO

Serves: 4   **Prep: 25–30 mins**   **Cook: 40–45 mins**

Ingredients

1 tbsp olive oil

40 g/1½ oz butter

1 small onion, finely chopped

225 g/8 oz pumpkin, diced

225 g/8 oz chestnuts, cooked and shelled

280 g/10 oz risotto rice

150 ml/5 fl oz dry white wine

1 tsp crumbled saffron threads (optional), dissolved in 4 tbsp of the stock

1 litre/1¾ pints simmering vegetable stock

85 g/3 oz Parmesan-style cheese, freshly grated, plus extra for serving

salt and pepper

Method

1 Heat the oil with 25 g/1 oz of the butter in a deep saucepan over a medium heat until the butter has melted. Stir in the onion and pumpkin and cook, stirring occasionally, for 5 minutes, or until the onion is soft and starting to turn golden and the pumpkin begins to colour.

2 Roughly chop the chestnuts and add to the mixture. Stir thoroughly to coat. Reduce the heat, add the rice and mix to coat in oil and butter. Cook, stirring constantly, for 2–3 minutes, or until the grains are translucent. Add the wine and cook, stirring constantly, for 1 minute, until it has reduced.

3 Add the saffron liquid to the rice, if using, and cook, stirring constantly, until the liquid has been absorbed. Gradually add the simmering stock, a ladleful at a time, stirring constantly. Add more liquid as the rice absorbs each addition. Increase the heat to medium so that the liquid bubbles.

4 Cook for 20 minutes, or until all the liquid has been absorbed and the rice is creamy. Season to taste with salt and pepper. Remove the risotto from the heat and add the remaining butter. Mix well, then stir in the cheese until it melts. Adjust the seasoning if necessary. Spoon the risotto onto four warmed plates and serve immediately, sprinkled with grated cheese.

DUCK WITH MADEIRA & BLUEBERRY SAUCE

Serves: 4

Prep: 25 mins, plus marinating

Cook: 15 mins, plus standing

Ingredients

4 duck breasts (skin left on)

4 garlic cloves, chopped

grated rind and juice of 1 orange

1 tbsp chopped fresh parsley

salt and pepper

selection of freshly cooked green vegetables, to serve

Madeira & blueberry sauce

150 g/5½ oz blueberries

250 ml/9 fl oz Madeira

1 tbsp redcurrant jelly

Method

1 Use a sharp knife to make several shallow diagonal cuts in each duck breast. Put the duck in a bowl with the garlic, orange rind and juice, and the parsley. Season to taste with salt and pepper and stir well. Turn the duck in the mixture until thoroughly coated. Cover the bowl with clingfilm and leave in the refrigerator to marinate for at least 1 hour.

2 Heat a dry, non-stick frying pan over a medium heat. Add the duck breasts and cook for 4 minutes, then turn them over and cook for a further 4 minutes, or according to taste. Remove from the heat, cover the frying pan and leave to stand for 5 minutes.

3 To make the sauce, halfway through the cooking time, put the blueberries, Madeira and redcurrant jelly into a separate saucepan. Bring to the boil. Reduce the heat and simmer for 10 minutes, then remove from the heat.

4 Slice the duck breasts and transfer to warmed serving plates. Serve with the sauce poured over and accompanied by a selection of green vegetables.

FAMILY CELEBRATION DINNERS

BLACK PUDDING WITH CARAMELIZED PEAR AND CIDER

Serves: 4　　　　**Prep: 25 mins**　　　　**Cook: 35–40 mins**

Ingredients

40 g/1½ oz
lightly salted butter

3 firm pears, such as
Conference, peeled, cored
and quartered lengthways

350 g/12 oz black pudding,
thickly sliced

2 shallots, chopped

125 ml/4 fl oz chicken stock

125 ml/4 fl oz dry cider

sea salt flakes

black pepper

125 ml/4 fl oz single cream

squeeze of lemon juice

3 tbsp chopped
fresh flat-leaf parsley

Method

1 Heat half of the butter in a heavy-based frying pan. When it sizzles, sauté the pear segments over a medium–low heat for 10 minutes, turning, until caramelized at the edges. Remove from the frying pan and keep warm.

2 Add the black pudding slices to the frying pan and cook for 3 minutes on each side side, turning them carefully so that they don't disintegrate. Set aside and keep warm.

3 Pour off the fat and wipe the frying pan clean with kitchen paper. Heat the remaining butter in the frying pan, add the shallots and cook for 3–4 minutes, until softened.

4 Pour in the stock and cider, raise the heat and bring to the boil. Reduce the heat a little, then simmer briskly for 5–7 minutes, until reduced by half. Season with sea salt and plenty of pepper.

5 Add the cream to the frying pan and simmer for about a minute, until slightly thickened.

6 Return the pear slices to the frying pan, add a squeeze of lemon and cook for a further minute or until heated through. Sprinkle with the parsley and serve with the black pudding slices.

RED CABBAGE STUFFED WITH MUSHROOMS, NUTS & RICE

Serves: 4–6   **Prep: 35–40 mins**   **Cook: 1¼ hours**

Ingredients

50 g/1¾ oz butter plus extra for greasing.

1 large red cabbage

juice of 2 lemons

3 tbsp olive oil

1 onion, chopped

150 g/5½ oz mushrooms, chopped

175 g/6 oz mixed nuts, chopped

3 garlic cloves, chopped

2 tbsp chopped fresh oregano

115 g/4 oz cooked Camargue red rice

300 ml/10 fl oz vegetable stock

sea salt and pepper

250 ml/9 fl oz tomato sauce (see page 82)

Method

1 Preheat the oven to 180°C/350°F/ Gas Mark 4. Grea a 1-litre/1¾-pint round ovenproof dish with butter. Bring a saucepan of lightly salted water to the boil. Remove 8–10 cabbage leaves and plunge into the boiling water. Add half the lemon juice and boil for 4 minutes. Drain and pat dry. Shave off the thickest pa of the stalk.

2 Cut the remaining cabbage in half lengthways reserving half for another recipe. Cut into quarters and discard the core. Shred the leaves Heat the oil and half the butter in a large frying pan over a medium heat. Add the onion and fr for 5 minutes, until translucent.

3 Add the mushrooms, nuts, chopped cabbage, garli oregano, and salt and pepper to taste and cook fo minutes. Stir in the rice, remaining lemon juice and h the stock and cook for a further 2 minutes.

4 Arrange the cabbage leaves around the edge and base of the prepared dish, leaving no gaps. Fill with the stuffing, pressing it in well. Dot with the remaining butter. Fold over the tops of the leaves Pour the remaining stock round the edge. Tightly cover with thick foil, and bake in the preheated oven for 45–50 minutes. Meanwhile, make the Tomato Sauce. Serve the cabbage in wedges, accompanied by the tomato sauce.

FAMILY CELEBRATION DINNERS

PERFECT ROAST POTATOES

Serves: 8   **Prep: 20 mins**   **Cook: 1 hour 25 mins**

Ingredients

70 g/2½ oz goose
or duck fat or
5 tbsp olive oil

1 kg/2 lb 4 oz even-sized
floury potatoes, such as
King Edward, Maris Piper
or Desirée

coarse sea salt

8 fresh rosemary sprigs,
to garnish

Method

1 Preheat the oven to 230°C/450°F/Gas Mark 8. P
the fat in a large roasting tin, sprinkle generously
with sea salt and place in the preheated oven.

2 Meanwhile, cook the potatoes in a large
saucepan of boiling water for 8–10 minutes unti
par-boiled. Drain well and, if the potatoes are
large, cut them in half. Return the potatoes to
the empty saucepan and shake vigorously to
roughen their outsides.

3 Arrange the potatoes in a single layer in the
hot fat and roast for 45 minutes. If they look as if
they are beginning to char around the edges,
reduce the oven temperature to 200°C/400°F/
Gas Mark 6. Turn the potatoes over and roast fo
a further 30 minutes until crisp. Serve garnished
with rosemary sprigs.

FAMILY CELEBRATION DINNERS

MINI YORKSHIRE PUDDINGS

Makes: 6   **Prep: 20 mins**   **Cook: 35–40 mins**

Ingredients

0 g/1 oz beef dripping or
2 tbsp sunflower oil

140 g/5 oz plain flour

½ tsp salt

2 eggs

225 ml/8 fl oz milk

Method

1 Grease six metal pudding moulds with the
   dripping, then divide the remaining dripping
   between the moulds. Preheat the oven to
   220°C/425°F/Gas Mark 7, placing the moulds
   in the oven so the dripping can melt while the
   oven heats.

2 Sift together the flour and salt into a large mixing
   bowl and make a well in the centre. Break
   the eggs into the well, add the milk and beat,
   gradually drawing in the flour from the side to
   make a smooth batter. Remove the moulds from
   the oven and spoon in the batter until they are
   about half full.

3 Bake in the preheated oven for 30–35 minutes
   without opening the door, until the puddings
   are well risen, puffed and golden brown. Serve
   immediately, as they will collapse if left to stand.

FAMILY CELEBRATION DINNERS

COCKLE & MUSSEL GRATIN

Serves: 3–4   **Prep: 30–35 mins**   **Cook: 25–30 mins**

Ingredients

750 g/1 lb 10 oz mussels

125 ml/4 fl oz water

115 g/4 oz lightly salted butter

2 onions, chopped

225 g/8 oz cooked shelled cockles

juice and finely grated zest of ½ lemon

3 tbsp chopped fresh parsley

100 g/3½ oz coarse breadcrumbs from a day-old ciabatta loaf

2 garlic cloves, finely chopped

salt and pepper

Method

1 Preheat the oven to 220°C/425°F/Gas Mark 7. Scrub and debeard the mussels, discarding any with broken shells or that remain open. Put in a large saucepan with the water. Cover and steam for 4–5 minutes, until the shells open. Discard any that remain closed. Reserve eight mussels in their shells as a garnish. Remove the rest from the shell.

2 Melt half the butter in a frying pan over a medium–high heat. Add the onions and sauté for 7 minutes, until soft but not coloured. Transfer to a 1.7-litre/3-pint gratin dish measuring 26 x 19 cm/10½ x 7½ inches.

3 Add the cockles, shelled mussels, lemon juice and 2 tablespoons of the parsley. Season with salt and pepper and stir to mix.

4 Set aside a knob of butter and melt the remaining butter. Mix with the breadcrumbs, garlic, lemon zest and remaining parsley. Season with a little more salt and pepper. Spread the breadcrumb mixture over the seafood. Top with the reserved mussels and dot them with the remaining butter.

5 Bake in the oven for 10–15 minutes, until the crumbs are golden and crisp and the seafood thoroughly heated. Serve immediately.

FAMILY CELEBRATION DINNERS

ROASTED CAULIFLOWER, TOMATO & OLIVE GRATIN

Serves: 4   **Prep: 30 mins**   **Cook: 1 hour 20 mins**

Ingredients

4 tbsp olive oil

50 g/1¾ oz butter, plus extra for greasing

1 large onion, chopped

1½ tsp fresh thyme leaves

3 garlic cloves, thinly sliced

800 g/1 lb 12 oz canned chopped tomatoes

2–3 slivers lemon peel

100 g/3½ oz coarse ciabatta breadcrumbs

10–12 Kalamata olives, pitted and chopped

4 tbsp chopped fresh flat-leaf parsley

1 large cauliflower

25 g/1 oz coarsely grated Parmesan-style cheese

sea salt and pepper

Method

1 Heat 2 tablespoons of the oil and half the butter in a high-sided frying pan over a medium heat. Add the onion and thyme and fry for 5 minutes, until the onion is translucent. Add the garlic and fry for 1–2 minutes, until just coloured.

2 Stir in the tomatoes and lemon peel. Season with salt and pepper, then simmer, stirring, for 20 minutes, until thickened.

3 Preheat the oven to 200°C/400°F/Gas Mark 6. Grease an ovenproof dish with butter. Combine the breadcrumbs, olives and parsley in a bowl. Mix in the remaining oil.

4 Cut the cauliflower into quarters. Cut out the core. Break the florets into clumps and pack in a single layer in the prepared dish. Season with salt and pepper.

5 Pour in the tomato sauce, pushing it into the spaces between the florets. Sprinkle the breadcrumb mixture evenly over the top. Dot with the remaining butter.

6 Cover with foil and roast in the preheated oven for 35 minutes. Remove the foil and roast for a further 15 minutes, until the cauliflower is tender-crisp and the crumbs are golden. Sprinkle with cheese and serve immediately.

CREAMED CHICKEN WITH JERUSALEM ARTICHOKES

Serves: 2   **Prep: 20 mins**   **Cook: 30 mins**

Ingredients

25 g/1 oz butter

1 onion, finely chopped

200 g/7 oz Jerusalem artichokes, sliced

200 ml/7 fl oz water

100 ml/3½ fl oz white wine

2 fresh tarragon sprigs or ½ tsp dried tarragon

2 skinless, boneless chicken breasts, about 115 g/4 oz each

1 tsp Dijon mustard

3 tbsp crème fraîche

salt and pepper

chopped fresh tarragon, to garnish (optional)

cooked rice, to serve

Method

1 Melt the butter in a large frying pan over a medium heat, add the onions and cook for 4–5 minutes, or until soft. Add the artichokes, water, wine and tarragon. Bring to the boil, then reduce the heat and simmer, covered, for 5 minutes, or until the artichokes are just tender.

2 Cut each chicken breast into 4 pieces and add to the pan. Season with salt and pepper and continue to cook, stirring, for 10 minutes, or until the chicken is cooked through and shows no traces of pink.

3 Remove the tarragon sprigs and stir in the mustard and crème fraîche. Increase the heat and leave the sauce to bubble and thicken. Divide between two warmed plates and garnish with chopped tarragon, if using. Serve immediately with cooked rice.

SLOW-ROAST SHOULDER OF LAMB WITH HERB DUMPLINGS

Serves: 4-6   **Prep: 40-45 mins**   **Cook: 3 hours 55 mins**

Ingredients

2 large carrots,
cut into thin sticks

1 onion, sliced

1.5 kg/3 lb 5 oz blade-end
bone-in shoulder of lamb

2-3 fresh bay leaves

1 sage sprig

small bunch parsley

600 ml/1 pint meat stock

salt and pepper

Herb-flavoured dumplings

115 g/4 oz plain flour

1 tsp baking powder

½ tsp salt

¼ tsp black pepper

1½ tbsp finely chopped
fresh parsley

1½ tbsp finely chopped fresh
mint or herb of your choice

25 g/1 oz lightly salted butter

1 egg

2 tbsp milk

Method

1 Preheat the oven to 230°C/450°F/Gas Mark 8. Scatter the carrots and onion in a roasting tin. Place the meat on top, tucking the herbs underneath. Season, then pour in enough stock to not quite cover the vegetables. Cover with foil, sealing the edges well. Roast for 20 minutes, the reduce the heat to 160°C/325°F/Gas Mark 3 and roast fo a further 3 hours.

2 To make the dumplings, sift the flour, baking powder and salt into a bowl. Mix in the pepper and herbs. Rub in the butter until the mixture resembles coarse breadcrumbs. Beat together the egg and milk in a jug, then stir into the flour mixture to make a soft, slightly sticky dough. With floured hands, divide the dough into 12 pieces and roll into balls. Drop into a large saucepan of boiling salted water. Partially cover and cook for 15 minutes. Using tongs, lift the dumplings into a colander to drain for a fev minutes. Transfer to a plate until needed.

3 Just before the meat is ready, heat the remaining stock a saucepan. Remove the meat from the oven. Open th foil. Arrange the dumplings around the meat and pour i the hot stock. Reseal the foil; roast for 15 minutes. Transfe the meat to a warmed platter and discard the herbs. Arrange the dumplings and vegetables around the me Strain the juices into a jug and serve with the meat.

★ Variation

Add extra flavour with a generous splash of red wir to the stock in step 3.

PERFECT PUDDINGS

STICKY TOFFEE PUDDING

Serves: 8

Prep: 25 mins,
plus soaking

Cook: 45–50 mins

Ingredients

75 g/2¾ oz sultanas

150 g/5½ oz dates, stoned and chopped

1 tsp bicarbonate of soda

25 g/1 oz butter, plus extra for greasing

200 g/7 oz soft light brown sugar

2 eggs

200 g/7 oz self-raising flour, sifted

Sticky toffee sauce

25 g/1 oz butter

175 ml/6 fl oz double cream

200 g/7 oz soft light brown sugar sifted

Method

1 Preheat the oven to 180°C/350°F/Gas Mark 4. Grease a 20-cm/8-inch round cake tin. To make the pudding, put the sultanas, dates and bicarbonate of soda into a heatproof bowl. Cover with boiling water and leave to soak. Put the butter into a separate bowl, add the sugar and mix well.

2 Beat the eggs into the butter mixture, then fold in the flour. Drain the soaked fruit, add to the bowl and mix. Spoon the mixture evenly into the prepared cake tin. Bake in the preheated oven for 35–40 minutes, or until a skewer inserted into the centre comes out clean.

3 About 5 minutes before the end of the cooking time, make the sauce. Melt the butter in a saucepan over a medium heat. Stir in the cream and sugar and bring to the boil, stirring constantly. Reduce the heat and simmer for 5 minutes. Cut the pudding into equal-sized portions, pour over the sauce and serve immediately.

★ Variation

For a contemporary twist, stir in 2 teaspoons of coffee granules when making the sticky toffee sauce.

LEMON MERINGUE PIE

Serves: 8

Prep: 40 mins, plus chilling and cooling

Cook: 1 hour

Ingredients

Pastry

150 g/5½ oz plain flour, plus extra for dusting

85 g/3 oz butter, cut into small pieces, plus extra for greasing

35 g/1¼ oz icing sugar, sifted

finely grated rind of ½ lemon

½ egg yolk, beaten

1½ tbsp milk

Filling

3 tbsp cornflour

300 ml/10 fl oz water

juice and grated rind of 2 lemons

175 g/6 oz caster sugar

2 eggs, separated

Method

1 To make the pastry, sift the flour into a bowl. Rub in the butter with your fingertips until the mixture resembles fine breadcrumbs. Mix in the remaining pastry ingredients. Turn out onto a lightly floured work surface and knead briefly. Roll into a ball, wrap in clingfilm and chill in the refrigerator for 30 minutes.

2 Preheat the oven to 180°C/350°F/Gas Mark 4. Grease a 20-cm/8-inch round tart tin. Roll out the pastry to a thickness of 5 mm/¼ inch, then use it to line the base and side of the tin. Prick all over with a fork, line with baking paper and fill with baking beans. Bake blind in the preheated oven for 15 minutes. Remove the pastry case from the oven and take out the paper and beans. Reduce the oven temperature to 150°C/300°F/Gas Mark 2.

3 To make the filling, mix the cornflour with a little of the water to form a paste. Put the remaining water in a saucepan. Stir in the lemon juice, lemon rind and cornflour paste. Bring to the boil, stirring. Cook for 2 minutes. Leave to cool slightly. Stir in 5 tablespoons of the caster sugar and the egg yolks, then pour into the pastry case.

4 Whisk the egg whites in a clean bowl until stiff. Gradually whisk in the remaining caster sugar and spread the meringue over the pie. Bake for a further 40 minutes. Remove from the oven, cool and serve.

TREACLE TART

Serves: 8

Prep: 30 mins,   **Cook: 35–40 mins**
plus chilling and cooling

Ingredients

250 g/9 oz ready-made shortcrust pastry

plain flour, for dusting

350 g/12 oz golden syrup

125 g/4½ oz fresh white breadcrumbs

125 ml/4 fl oz double cream

finely grated rind of ½ lemon or orange

2 tbsp lemon juice or orange juice

whipped cream or clotted cream, to serve

Method

1 Roll out the pastry on a lightly floured work surface and use to line a 20-cm/8-inch tart tin, reserving the pastry trimmings. Prick the base of the pastry case all over with a fork, cover with clingfilm and chill in the refrigerator for 30 minutes. Re-roll the reserved pastry trimmings and cut out small shapes, such as leaves, stars or hearts, to decorate the top of the tart.

2 Preheat the oven to 190°C/375°F/Gas Mark 5. Mix the golden syrup, breadcrumbs, double cream and lemon rind with the lemon juice in small bowl.

3 Pour the mixture into the pastry case and decorate the top of the tart with the pastry shapes of your choice. Transfer to the preheated oven and bake for 35–40 minutes, or until the filling is just set.

4 Leave the tart to cool slightly before serving. Cut into wedges and serve with cream.

HEDGEROW FRUIT CRUMBLE

Serves: 6 **Prep: 25 mins** **Cook: 50–55 mins**

Ingredients

500 g/1 lb 2 oz cooking apples (two large ones), peeled and cut into bite-sized chunks

150-g/5½ oz blackberries

25 g/1 oz elderberries or blackcurrants

40 g/1½ oz demerara sugar

½ tsp ground cinnamon

1 tbsp water

Crumble topping

175 g/6 oz plain flour

25 g/1 oz rolled oats

85 g/3 oz butter, diced

85 g/3 oz demerara sugar

55 g/2 oz hazelnuts, chopped

1 tbsp lemon juice

Method

1 Preheat the oven to 190°C/375°F/Gas Mark 5. Place the apples, blackberries and elderberries in a 1.2-litre/2-pint baking dish. Stir in the sugar, cinnamon and water. Cover tightly with foil and bake in the preheated oven for 30 minutes until the apples are softened but not cooked right through.

2 For the crumble topping, mix the flour and oats together in a bowl. Add the butter and rub in with your fingertips until the mixture resembles fine breadcrumbs. Stir in the sugar and hazelnuts.

3 Remove the foil from the baked fruit and stir. Sprinkle the crumble mixture evenly over the top. Return to the oven for 20–25 minutes until lightly browned and starting to bubble at the edges. Serve immediately.

IRISH WHISKEY TRIFLE

Serves: 8

Prep: 35–40 mins, plus **Cook: 10 mins**
cooling, soaking & chilling

Ingredients

10 sponge fingers
or 1 stale sponge cake

raspberry jam, for spreading

2 macaroons,
lightly crushed

finely grated zest of 1 lemon

2 tbsp Irish whiskey

125 ml/4 fl oz sherry

300 ml/10 fl oz double
cream

½ tbsp sugar

150 g/5½ oz raspberries

miniature macaroons or
candied violets, to decorate

Custard

5 egg yolks, lightly beaten

50 g/1¾ oz caster sugar

2 tsp cornflour

125 ml/4 fl oz full fat milk

250 ml/9 fl oz double cream

½ tsp vanilla extract

Method

1 First make the custard. Combine the egg yolks
and sugar in a mixing bowl. Stir in the cornflour
and mix to a smooth paste, then whisk in the milk.

2 Heat the cream in a heavy-based saucepan
until just starting to simmer but not boiling.
Gradually whisk the hot cream into the egg
mixture, then return the mixture to the pan. Whisk
constantly over a medium heat for about 5
minutes, until thickened. Immediately pour into
a jug and stir in the vanilla extract. Cover with
clingfilm to prevent a skin forming and leave to
cool completely.

3 Thickly spread half of the sponge fingers with
raspberry jam. Place the remaining sponge
fingers on top to make a sandwich. If using
sponge cake, slice horizontally into two or three
layers and spread with jam. Arrange in a single
layer in the base of a deep serving dish. Sprinkle
with the crushed macaroons and the lemon zest.

4 Combine the whiskey and sherry and pour over the
sponge finger mixture. Leave to soak for 1 hour.

Spoon the cooled custard over the sponge finger mixture.

Whip the cream with the sugar until stiff peaks form. Spread over the custard, levelling with a palette knife. Cover with clingfilm and chill for 1 hour, or until ready to serve.

Arrange the raspberries on top and decorate with miniature macaroons or candied violets.

CHOCOLATE PUDDING

Serves: 6

Prep: 20–25 mins, plus optional cooling & chilling

Cook: 10–15 mins

Ingredients

100 g/3½ oz sugar
4 tbsp cocoa powder
2 tbsp cornflour
pinch of salt
350 ml/12 fl oz milk
1 egg, beaten
55 g/2 oz butter
½ tsp vanilla extract
double cream, to serve

Method

1 Put the sugar, cocoa powder, cornflour and salt into a heatproof bowl. Stir and set aside.

2 Pour the milk into a saucepan and heat over a medium heat until just simmering. Do not bring to the boil.

3 Keeping the pan over a medium heat, spoon a little of the simmering milk into the sugar mixture and blend, then stir this mixture into the milk in the pan. Beat in the egg and half of the butter and reduce the heat to low.

4 Simmer for 5–8 minutes, stirring frequently, until the mixture thickens. Remove from the heat and add the vanilla extract and the remaining butter, stirring until the butter melts and is absorbed.

5 The pudding can be served hot or chilled, with cream for pouring over. If chilling the pudding, spoon it into a serving bowl and leave to cool, then press clingfilm onto the surface to prevent a skin forming and chill in the refrigerator until required.

PERFECT PUDDINGS

LEMON & LIME POSSET

Serves: 4

Prep: 20 mins, plus
cooling and chilling

Cook: 8 mins

Ingredients

500 ml/18 fl oz
double cream

140 g/5 oz caster sugar

finely grated rind and juice
of 1 large lemon

finely grated rind
and juice of 1 lime,
plus extra rind to serve

200 g/7 oz strawberries,
hulled and halved

shortbread biscuits, to serve

Method

1 Place the cream and sugar in a saucepan. Bring slowly to the boil and simmer for 3 minutes, stirring occasionally.

2 Remove from the heat, add the lemon and lime rind and juices and whisk well. Pour into four glasses, leave to cool then cover and place in the refrigerator for about 2–3 hours until set and well chilled.

3 Divide the strawberries and extra lime rind between the glasses and serve with shortbread biscuits.

PERFECT PUDDINGS

SYRUP SPONGE WITH CUSTARD

Serves: 4   **Prep: 20 mins**   **Cook: 4 mins, plus standing**

Ingredients

4 tbsp golden syrup

125 g/4½ oz butter, plus extra for greasing

85 g/3 oz caster sugar

2 eggs, lightly beaten

125 g/4½ oz self-raising flour

1 tsp baking powder

about 2 tbsp warm water

ready-made custard, to serve

Method

1 Grease a 1.5-litre/2¾-pint pudding basin or microwave-safe bowl with butter. Spoon the golden syrup into the prepared basin.

2 Beat the butter with the sugar in a bowl until pale and fluffy. Gradually add the eggs, beating well after each addition.

3 Sift together the flour and baking powder, then gently fold into the butter mixture. Add enough water to give a soft, dropping consistency. Spoon the mixture into the basin and level the surface.

4 Cover with microwave-safe clingfilm, leaving a small space to let the air escape. Cook in a microwave oven on high for 4 minutes, then remove and leave the pudding to stand for 5 minutes while it continues to cook.

5 Turn out the pudding onto a serving plate. Serve immediately with custard.

2

RHUB

172

Serves: 6

Ingredien

900 g/2 lb th

115 g/4 oz cas
grated rind o

cream, yo

...ARB CRUMBLE

Prep: 25 mins   **Cook: 25–30 mins**

...ts

...ubarb
...er sugar
...d juice of
1 orange
...urt or custard,
to serve

Crumble topping

225 g/8 oz plain flour or
wholemeal flour
115 g/4 oz unsalted butter
115 g/4 oz soft light
brown sugar
1 tsp ground ginger

Method

1 Preheat the oven to 190°C/375°F/Gas Mark 5.

2 Cut the rhubarb into 2.5-cm/1-inch lengths and place in a 1.7-litre/3-pint ovenproof dish with the sugar and the orange rind and juice.

3 Make the crumble topping by placing the flour in a mixing bowl and rubbing in the butter until the mixture resembles breadcrumbs. Stir in the sugar and the ginger.

4 Spread the crumble evenly over the fruit and press down lightly using a fork. Bake in the centre of the preheated oven on a baking tray for 25–30 minutes until the crumble is golden brown. Serve with cream.

STRAWBERRY ICE CREAM SUNDAE

Serves: 4   **Prep: 20–25 mins**   **Cook: no cooking**

Ingredients

450 g/1 lb strawberries, hulled

2 tbsp icing sugar

1 tbsp lemon juice

150 ml/5 fl oz whipping cream

500 ml/18 fl oz vanilla ice cream

4 tbsp chopped blanched almonds, toasted

Method

1 Place 175 g/6 oz of the strawberries in a bowl with the sugar and lemon juice and purée with an electric hand-held blender until smooth.

2 Rub the purée through a fine sieve into a bowl, and discard the pips.

3 Whip the cream until thick enough to hold soft peaks. Slice the remaining strawberries. Layer the strawberries, scoops of ice cream and spoonfuls of cream in four glasses.

4 Spoon the purée over the sundaes and sprinkle with chopped almonds. Serve immediately.

WHISKY FUDGE

Makes: 16 approx. pieces

Prep: 25–30 mins, plus cooling, chilling & storing

Cook: 20–25 mins

Ingredients

a little sunflower oil, for greasing

250 g/9 oz soft brown sugar

100 g/3½ oz unsalted butter, diced

400 g/14 oz canned sweetened full-fat condensed milk

2 tbsp glucose syrup

150 g/5½ oz plain chocolate, roughly chopped

60 ml/2¼ fl oz Scotch whisky

25 g/1 oz walnut pieces

Method

1 Lightly brush a 20-cm/8-inch square baking tin with oil. Line it with non-stick baking paper, snipping diagonally into the corners, then pressing the paper into the tin so that the base and sides are lined. Put the sugar, butter, condensed milk and glucose into a heavy-based saucepan. Heat gently, stirring, until the sugar has dissolved.

2 Increase the heat and boil for 12–15 minutes, or until the mixture reaches 116°C/240°F on a sugar thermometer (if you don't have a sugar thermometer, spoon a little of the syrup into some iced water; it will form a soft ball when it is ready). As the temperature rises, stir the fudge occasionally so the sugar doesn't stick and burn. Remove the fudge from the heat. Add the chocolate and whisky and stir together until the chocolate has melted and the mixture is smooth.

3 Preheat the grill to medium–hot. Put the walnuts on a baking tray and toast them under the grill for 2–3 minutes, or until browned. Roughly chop them. Pour the mixture into the prepared baking tin, smooth the surface using a spatula and sprinkle over the walnuts. Leave to cool for 1 hour. Cover with cling film, then chill in the fridge for 1–2 hours, or until firm. Lift the fudge out of the tin, peel off the paper and cut into small squares. Store in an airtight container in a cool, dry place for up to 2 weeks.

PERFECT PUDDINGS

PEANUT BRITTLE

**Makes: about
500 g/1 lb 2 oz**

Prep: 25 mins,
plus cooling

Cook: 15 mins

Ingredients

vegetable or sunflower oil,
for oiling

200 g/7 oz granulated sugar

85 g/3 oz soft light
brown sugar

85 g/3 oz golden syrup

25 g/1 oz butter

6 tbsp water

175 g/6 oz salted peanuts,
roughly chopped

1 tsp vanilla extract

¼ tsp bicarbonate of soda

Method

1 Preheat the oven to 120°C/250°F/Gas Mark ½.
   Line a 30-cm/12-inch square baking pan with
   foil and oil lightly. Place in the preheated oven
   to warm.

2 Meanwhile, place the sugars, golden syrup,
   butter and water in a heavy-based saucepan.
   Heat gently, stirring until the butter has melted
   and the sugar has completely dissolved.

3 Brush around the inside of the pan above the
   level of the syrup with a pastry brush dipped
   in water, then turn up the heat and boil rapidly
   until the syrup reaches 150°C/300°F ('hard crack'
   stage).

4 Working quickly, remove from the heat and stir
   in the peanuts followed by the vanilla extract
   and bicarbonate of soda. Pour onto the warme
   baking tray and tip gently to level the surface.
   Leave for about 30 minutes to cool, then snap
   into pieces. Store in airtight bags or containers.

PERFECT PUDDINGS

PEPPERMINT CREAMS

Makes: 25

Prep: 25–30 mins plus chilling, setting & storing

Cook: 5 mins

Ingredients

1 large egg white

325 g/11½ oz icing sugar, sifted, plus extra for dipping if needed

a few drops of peppermint extract

a few drops of green food colouring

100 g/3½ oz plain chocolate, roughly chopped

Method

1 Line a baking tray with non-stick baking paper.

2 Lightly whisk the egg white in a large, clean mixing bowl until it is frothy but still translucent.

3 Add the sifted icing sugar to the egg white and stir using a wooden spoon until the mixture is stiff. Knead in the peppermint extract and food colouring.

4 Using the palms of your hands, roll the mixture into walnut sized balls and place them on the prepared baking tray. Use a fork to flatten them; if it sticks to them, dip it in icing sugar before pressing. Put the creams in the fridge to set for 24 hours.

5 Put the chocolate in a heatproof bowl, set the bowl over a saucepan of gently simmering water and heat until melted. Dip the creams halfway in the chocolate and return to the baking tray for 1 hour, or until set. Store in an airtight container in the fridge for up to 5 days.

PERFECT PUDDINGS

NUT FUDGE

Makes: 80 pieces approx.

Prep: 25 mins, plus cooling

Cook: 20 mins

Ingredients

300 ml/10 fl oz milk

1 kg/2 lb 4 oz golden granulated sugar

250 g/9 oz butter, plus extra for greasing

2 tbsp instant coffee granules

2 tbsp cocoa powder

2 tbsp golden syrup

400 g/14 oz canned condensed milk

115 g/4 oz shelled pecan nuts, chopped

Method

1 Grease a 30 x 23-cm/12 x 9-inch Swiss roll tin. Place the milk, sugar and butter in a large saucepan. Stir over a gentle heat until the sugar has dissolved. Stir in the coffee granules, cocoa, golden syrup and condensed milk.

2 Bring to the boil and boil steadily, whisking constantly, for 10 minutes, or until a little of the mixture, dropped into a small bowl of cold water forms a soft ball when rolled between the fingers.

3 Cool for 5 minutes, then beat vigorously with a wooden spoon until the mixture starts to thicken. Stir in the nuts. Continue beating until the mixture becomes thick, creamy and grainy. Quickly pour into the prepared tin and stand in a cool place to set. Cut the fudge into squares to serve.

COCONUT ICE

Makes: 50 pieces approx.

Prep: 25–30 mins, plus setting

Cook: No cooking

Ingredients

oil, for greasing

400 g/14 oz canned condensed milk

1 tsp vanilla extract

300 g/10½ oz desiccated coconut

300 g/10½ oz icing sugar

1 tbsp cocoa powder, sifted

few drops of red or pink food colouring (optional)

Method

1 Grease the base of a shallow 18-cm/7-inch square cake tin and line with baking paper. Mix the condensed milk and vanilla extract together in a large bowl. Add the coconut and icing sugar. Mix together with a wooden spoon until the mixture becomes very stiff.

2 Transfer half of the mixture to another bowl. Add the cocoa powder and mix well until it is an even colour. Spread over the base of the prepared tin and press down with the back of a spoon.

3 If using food colouring, mix a few drops into the remaining bowl of mixture until evenly pink in colour. Spread over the chocolate layer and smooth the top. Leave to set overnight before turning out and cutting into squares.

PERFECT PUDDINGS

IRISH BUTTERMILK PANCAKES

Makes: 12

Prep: 25 mins,
plus standing

Cook: 15–20 mins

Ingredients

175 g/6 oz plain flour

¾ tbsp sugar

½ tsp salt

1 tsp bicarbonate of soda

1 egg, lightly beaten

375 ml/13 fl oz buttermilk

3 tbsp vegetable oil, plus
extra for brushing

To serve

150 ml/5 fl oz whipping
cream, whipped

125 g/4½ oz blueberries

Method

1 Sift the flour, sugar, salt and bicarbonate of soda into a mixing bowl.

2 Mix the egg with the buttermilk and vegetable oil in a large jug. Add to the dry ingredients, beating to a smooth, creamy batter. Leave to stand for at least 30 minutes or up to 2 hours.

3 Heat a non-stick pancake pan or frying pan over a medium heat and brush with vegetable oil. Pour in enough batter to make 10-cm/4-inch rounds (about 50 ml/2 fl oz per pancake). Cook for 1½–2 minutes per side, or until small bubbles appear on the surface. Transfer to a dish and keep warm while you cook the rest.

4 Serve with softly whipped cream and blueberries

CHOCOLATE & STOUT ICE CREAM

Makes: about 850ml/ 1½ pints

Prep: 35–40 mins, plus cooling, chilling & freezing

Cook: 25 mins

Ingredients

375 ml/13 fl oz full fat milk

150 g/5½ oz sugar

150 g/5½ oz dark chocolate (at least 85% cocoa solids), broken into small pieces

4 egg yolks

1 tsp vanilla extract

325 ml/11 fl oz stout

250 ml/9 fl oz double cream

grated chocolate, to decorate

Method

1 Pour the milk into a saucepan and add the sugar. Bring to the boil, stirring, until the sugar has dissolved. Remove from the heat and stir in the chocolate.

2 Pour the egg yolks into a heatproof bowl and beat for 5 minutes, or until the whisk leaves a faint trail when lifted from the mixture. Stir some of the warm chocolate mixture into the egg yolks, then gradually beat in the rest.

3 Place the bowl over a saucepan of gently boiling water. Stir constantly for about 10 minutes until the mixture reaches a temperature of 85°C/185°F, or is thick enough to coat the back of a spoon. Take care not to allow it boil.

4 Strain the mixture through a fine sieve into a jug. Stir in the vanilla extract. Sit the base of the jug in iced water until cold, then cover with clingfilm and chill for 2 hours.

5 Meanwhile, pour the stout into a saucepan and bring to the boil. Reduce the heat and simmer briskly for 8 minutes, until reduced to 250 ml/9 fl oz. Pour into a jug, leave to cool, then chill in the refrigerator.

6 Stir the cream and chilled stout into the chocolate mixture, mixing well. Pour the mixture

into the bowl of an ice cream machine. Churn and freeze following the manufacturer's instructions. Alternatively, pour the mixture into a shallow freezerproof container, cover with clingfilm and freeze for about 2 hours, until beginning to harden around the edges. Beat until smooth to get rid of any ioo crystals. Freeze again, repeat the process twice, then freeze until completely firm.

7 Move the ice cream to the refrigerator 30 minutes before serving, to soften. Serve in chilled dishes, sprinkled with grated chocolate.

PROFITEROLES

Serves: 4

Prep: 40–45 mins, plus cooling

Cook: 35 mins

Ingredients

choux pastry

70 g/2½ oz
unsalted butter,
plus extra for greasing

200 ml/7 fl oz water

100 g/3½ oz plain flour

3 eggs, beaten

Cream filling

300 ml/10 fl oz
double cream

3 tbsp caster sugar

1 tsp vanilla extract

Chocolate & brandy
sauce

125 g/4½ oz
plain chocolate,
broken into small pieces

35 g/1¼ oz unsalted butter

6 tbsp water

2 tbsp brandy

Method

1 Preheat the oven to 200°C/400°F/Gas Mark 6.
Grease several large baking sheets.

2 To make the pastry, place the butter and water in
a saucepan and bring to the boil. Meanwhile, sift
the flour into a bowl. Turn off the heat and beat
in the flour until smooth. Cool for 5 minutes. Beat
in enough of the eggs to give the mixture a soft,
dropping consistency.

3 Transfer to a piping bag fitted with a 1-cm/½ -inch
plain nozzle. Pipe small balls onto the prepared
baking sheets. Bake in the preheated oven for 25
minutes. Remove from the oven. Pierce each ball
with a skewer to let the steam escape.

4 To make the filling, whip the cream, sugar and
vanilla extract together. Cut the pastry balls
across the middle, then fill with cream.

5 To make the sauce, gently melt the chocolate,
butter and water together in a small saucepan,
stirring constantly, until smooth. Stir in the brandy.

6 Pile the profiteroles into individual serving dishes,
pour over the sauce and serve.

CHOCOLATE ORANGE TART

Serves: 6

Prep: 35 mins,
plus chilling and cooling

Cook: 40–50 mins

Ingredients

200 g/7 oz ready-made sweet pastry

100 g/3½ plain chocolate, at least 70 per cent cocoa solids, broken into pieces

55 g/2 oz butter, cut into pieces

85 g/3 oz soft light brown sugar

2 large eggs

finely grated zest of 1 large orange

30 g/1 oz plain flour, plus extra for dusting

3 tbsp orange juice

2 clementines, peeled and thinly sliced (optional), and cocoa powder, to decorate

crème fraîche, to serve

Method

1 Thinly roll out the pastry on a lightly floured surface and use to line a 22-cm/8½-inch tart tin. Chill for 20 minutes.

2 Meanwhile, preheat the oven to 200°C/400°F/ Gas Mark 6. Line the pastry case with baking paper and fill with ceramic baking beans. Bake the preheated oven for 15 minutes, then remove the beans and paper and return to the oven for a further 5–10 minutes to crisp the base.

3 Put the chocolate and butter in a heatproof bowl set over a saucepan of gently simmering water and heat, stirring occasionally, until melted and smooth. Place the sugar, eggs and orange zest in a separate bowl and whisk together until frothy and the sugar has dissolved completely. S the flour over the top. Add the melted chocolat mixture and the orange juice and stir together until completely smooth.

4 Pour into the pastry case and return to the over for 15–20 minutes until the filling is just set in the middle. Cool for at least 30 minutes, then remov from the tin. Serve warm or chill overnight – the filling will become dense and truffle-like. To serve sift a little cocoa powder over the top of the ta and decorate with sliced clementines, if using. Serve with crème fraîche.

BOOZY SUMMER PUDDING

Serves: 6

Prep: 35 mins,
plus chilling

Cook: 3–4 mins

Ingredients

600 g/1 lb 5 oz mixed
redcurrants, blackcurrants,
blueberries and raspberries,
plus extra to decorate
(optional)

3–4 tbsp caster sugar

6 tbsp port

300 g/10½ oz strawberries,
hulled and halved or
quartered if large

6–7 slices thick white bread,
crusts removed

double cream, to serve

Method

1 Remove the currants from their stems and place in a saucepan with the rest of the fruit (except the strawberries), two tablespoons of the sugar and half the port. Simmer gently for 3–4 minutes until the fruit starts to release its juices. Remove from the heat. Add the strawberries and stir in the remaining sugar to taste.

2 Line a 1-litre/1¾-pint pudding basin with clingfilm, letting the ends overhang. Tip the fruit into a sieve set over a bowl to catch the juices, then stir the remaining port into the juices. Cut a circle the same size as the bottom of one slice of bread. Dip in the juice mixture to coat and place in the bottom of the basin.

3 Reserve one slice of bread. Cut the rest in half slightly on an angle. Dip the pieces one at a time in the juice mixture and place around the sides of the basin, narrowest end down, pushing them together so there aren't any gaps and trimming the final piece of bread to fit (and any other pieces that are overhanging and need trimming.

4 Fill with the fruit then cover with the reserved piece of bread, cut to fit the top of the basin. Put a small plate on top and weigh it down with a

PERFECT PUDDINGS

can or two. Some juices may escape so place the basin on a plate to catch any spills. Chill overnight in the refrigerator. Set aside any remaining juice in the refrigerator.

Remove the weight and plate, then cover the pudding with a plate and flip over. Remove the bowl and clingfilm and decorate with extra summer fruits (if using). Serve with any remaining juice and cream.

IRISH CREAM CHEESECAKE

Serves: 8

Prep: 30 mins,   **Cook: 10 mins**
plus chilling and cooling

Ingredients

vegetable oil, for oiling

175 g/6 oz chocolate chip cookies

55 g/2 oz unsalted butter

crème fraîche and fresh strawberries, to serve

Filling

225 g/8 oz plain chocolate, broken into pieces

225 g/8 oz milk chocolate, broken into pieces

55 g/2 oz golden caster sugar

350 g/12 oz cream cheese

425 ml/15 fl oz double cream, lightly whipped

3 tbsp Irish Cream liqueur

Method

1 Line the base of a 20-cm/8-inch round springform cake tin with baking paper and brush the sides with oil. Place the cookies in a polythene bag and crush with a rolling pin. Put the butter in a saucepan and heat gently until melted. Stir in the crushed cookies. Press into the base of the prepared cake tin and chill in the refrigerator for 1 hour.

2 Put the plain and milk chocolate into a heatproof bowl set over a saucepan of gently simmering water until melted. Leave to cool. Put the sugar and cream cheese in a bowl and beat together until smooth, then fold in the cream. Fold the melted chocolate into the cream cheese mixture, then stir in the liqueur.

3 Spoon into the cake tin and smooth the surface. Leave to chill in the refrigerator for 2 hours, or until quite firm. Transfer to a serving plate and cut into slices. Serve with crème fraîche and strawberries.

CHOCOLATE BREAD PUDDING

Serves: 4

Prep: 30 mins,
plus chilling and standing

Cook: 45–50 mins

Ingredients

6 slices thick white bread, crusts removed

450 ml/16 fl oz milk

175 ml/6 fl oz canned evaporated milk

2 tbsp cocoa powder

2 eggs

2 tbsp brown sugar

1 tsp vanilla extract

icing sugar, for dusting

Hot fudge sauce

55 g/2 oz plain chocolate, broken into pieces

1 tbsp cocoa powder

2 tbsp golden syrup

55 g/2 oz butter or margarine, plus extra for greasing

2 tbsp brown sugar

150 ml/5 fl oz milk

1 tbsp cornflour

Method

1 Grease a shallow ovenproof baking dish. Cut the bread into squares and layer them in the dish.

2 Put the milk, evaporated milk and cocoa powder in a saucepan and heat gently, stirring occasional until the mixture is lukewarm. Whisk the eggs, sugar and vanilla extract together in a large jug. Add the warm milk mixture and beat well.

3 Pour into the prepared dish, making sure that all the bread is completely covered. Cover the dish with clingfilm and chill in the refrigerator for 1–2 hours, then bake in a preheated oven, 180°C/350°F/Gas Mark 4, for 35–40 minutes, until set. Leave to stand for 5 minutes.

4 To make the sauce, put all the ingredients into a saucepan and heat gently, stirring constantly until smooth.

5 Dust the chocolate bread pudding with icing sug and serve immediately with the hot fudge sauce.

GOOSEBERRY FOOL

Serves: 4

Prep: 25 mins,
plus cooling & chilling

Cook: 15 mins

Ingredients

300 g/10½ oz gooseberries, topped and tailed

4 tbsp caster sugar

finely grated zest of 1 lime

1 tbsp water

250 ml/9 fl oz double cream

125 ml/4 fl oz elderflower cordial

shortbread biscuits and lime rind, to serve

Method

1 Place the gooseberries in a saucepan with the sugar, lime zest and water. Heat until simmering then cover and cook for 10 minutes until the fruit bursts.

2 Transfer to a bowl and crush the fruit against the side of the bowl with a fork. Leave to cool completely then chill for 20 minutes.

3 Whisk the cream and elderflower cordial together with an electric whisk until the mixture holds its shape, then fold in the gooseberries. Spoon into four small glasses. Serve chilled with shortbread biscuits and decorated with lime rind

PERFECT PUDDINGS

CHOCOLATE & BANANA SUNDAE

Serves: 4   **Prep: 30 mins**   **Cook: 5 mins**

Ingredients

Chocolate Sauce

5 g/2 oz plain chocolate

4 tbsp golden syrup

15 g/½ oz butter

tbsp brandy or dark rum (optional)

Sundae

ml/5 fl oz double cream

4 bananas, peeled

scoops vanilla ice cream

g/2¾ oz chopped mixed nuts, toasted

40 g/1½ oz milk or plain chocolate, grated

4 fan wafers, to serve

Method

1 To make the chocolate sauce, break the chocolate into small pieces and place in a heatproof bowl with the golden syrup and butter. Set over a saucepan of gently simmering water until melted, stirring until well combined. Remove the bowl from the heat and stir in the brandy, if using.

2 To make the sundae, whip the cream until just holding its shape and slice the bananas. Place a scoop of ice cream in the bottom of each of four tall sundae glasses. Top with slices of banana, some chocolate sauce, a spoonful of cream and a generous sprinkling of nuts.

3 Repeat the layers, finishing with a good dollop of cream, then sprinkle with the remaining nuts and the grated chocolate. Serve with fan wafers.

KNICKERBOCKER GLORY

Serves: 4

Prep: 30 mins,
plus cooling

Cook: 7–10 mins

Ingredients

Melba sauce

175 g/6 oz raspberries

1½ tbsp icing sugar, sifted

Chocolate sauce

40 g/1½ oz plain chocolate, chopped

1 tbsp soft light brown sugar

100 ml/3½ fl oz milk

Filling

450 g/1 lb prepared fresh fruit (e.g. sliced banana, seedless grapes, hulled and halved strawberries, pineapple chunks, chopped nectarines, raspberries)

700 ml/1¼ pints vanilla ice cream (9 small scoops)

Topping

200 ml/7 fl oz double cream, softly whipped

15 g/½ oz chopped mixed nuts, lightly toasted

4 fan wafers

4 pitted fresh cherries or maraschino cherries

Method

1 To make the Melba sauce, place the raspberries and icing sugar in a food processor and blend to a purée. Rub through a sieve and discard the pips.

2 To make the chocolate sauce, place all the ingredients in a small, heavy-based saucepan and heat gently until melted. Stir well and simmer for 2 minutes. Cool.

3 Assemble the Knickerbocker Glory just before serving. Spoon alternate layers of fruit, ice cream and Melba sauce into four tall sundae glasses, filling them almost to the top.

4 Top each glass with a spoonful of cream, then drizzle with the chocolate sauce and sprinkle nuts on top. Add a wafer to each glass and finish with a cherry. Serve immediately

QUEEN OF PUDDINGS WITH BERRY FRUITS

Serves: 6

Prep: 30–35 mins, plus cooling

Cook: 55–60 mins

Ingredients

600 ml/1 pint milk

25 g/1 oz butter, plus extra for greasing

finely grated rind of 1 lemon

140 g/5 oz caster sugar

115 g/4 oz fresh white breadcrumbs

4 large eggs, separated

3 tbsp raspberry conserve or jam, warmed

125 g/4½ oz blueberries

125 g/4½ oz raspberries

single cream, to serve

Method

1 Place the milk, butter and lemon rind in a saucepan. Heat to simmering point then add in 25 g/1 oz of the sugar and stir to dissolve. Remove from the heat and stir in the breadcrumbs. Leave to cool and soften the breadcrumbs for 20 minutes.

2 Preheat the oven to 160°C/325°F/Gas Mark 3. Whisk the egg yolks into the breadcrumb mixture and pour into a lightly greased 1.2-litre/2-pint baking dish. Bake in the preheated oven for 40 minutes or until just set in the middle. Leave the oven on.

3 Spread the conserve over the top of the pudding, being careful not to break the surface too much. Mix the blueberries and raspberries together and scatter over the top.

4 Place the egg whites in a clean bowl and whisk with an electric whisk until stiff peaks form. Slowly beat in the remaining sugar, one tablespoon at a time, until the meringue is thick and glossy. Spoon over the pudding, covering the top completely, and return to the oven for 10–15 minutes until just browned. Serve immediately with cream.

BLACKBERRY SOUP WITH BUTTERMILK CUSTARDS

Serves: 4

Prep: 30 mins, plus soaking, chilling & cooling

Cook: 15 mins

Ingredients

Buttermilk Custards

4 sheets leaf gelatine

275 ml/9½ fl oz buttermilk

275 ml/9½ fl oz double cream

50 ml/2 fl oz milk

100 g/3½ oz caster sugar

Blackberry Soup

450 g/1 lb blackberries

300 ml/10 fl oz fruity red wine

100 ml/3½ fl oz water

75 g/2¾ oz caster sugar, or to taste

2 star anise

4–5 tbsp blackberry liqueur (optional)

Method

1 To make the custards, put the gelatine in a small bowl, cover with cold water and leave to soak for 5 minutes. Meanwhile, heat the buttermilk, cream and milk together in a saucepan to just below boiling point. Add the sugar and stir until it has completely dissolved. Remove the gelatine from the soaking liquid and squeeze out any excess water. Add to the hot buttermilk mixture and stir until completely dissolved. Pour through a fine sieve and fill four dariole moulds or individual pudding moulds. Transfer to the refrigerator and chill for several hours, or overnight, until set.

2 To make the blackberry soup, put the blackberries, wine and water in a large saucepan with the sugar and star anise. Simmer very gently for 8–10 minutes, until the sugar has dissolved and the mixture has a lovely anise scent. Remove from the heat and leave to cool. Once the mixture has cooled, remove and discard the star anise, transfer the mixture to a food processor and blend until smooth. Pour through a fine sieve and stir in the liqueur, if using. Cover and chill in the refrigerator until ready to serve.

3 To serve, divide the blackberry soup between four soup plates (rather than deep bowls) and place a buttermilk custard in the centre of each.

PERFECT PUDDINGS

LATTICED CHERRY PIE

Serves: 8

Prep: 40 mins,
plus chilling

Cook: 55 mins

Ingredients

Pastry

140 g/5 oz plain flour,
plus extra for dusting

¼ tsp baking powder

½ tsp mixed spice

½ tsp salt

50 g/1¾ oz caster sugar

55 g/2 oz unsalted butter,
chilled and diced,
plus extra for greasing

1 egg, beaten,
plus extra for glazing

Filling

900 g/2 lb stoned fresh
cherries, or canned cherries,
drained

150 g/5½ oz caster sugar

½ tsp almond extract

2 tsp cherry brandy

¼ tsp mixed spice

2 tbsp cornflour

2 tbsp water

25 g/1 oz unsalted butter,
melted

ice cream, to serve

Method

1 To make the pastry, sift the flour with the baking powder into a large bowl. Stir in the mixed spice, salt and sugar. Rub in the butter until the mixture resembles fine breadcrumbs, make a well in the centre, pour in the egg and mix into a dough. Cut the dough in half, and roll each half into a ball. Wrap in clingfilm and chill in the refrigerator for 30 minutes. Preheat the oven to 220°C/425°F/Gas Mark 7. Grease a 23-cm/9-inch pie dish. Roll out the doughs into two rounds, each 30 cm/12 inches in diameter. Use one to line the pie dish.

2 To make the filling, put half the cherries and all the sugar in a saucepan. Bring to a simmer and stir in the almond extract, brandy and mixed spice. In a bowl, mix the cornflour and water. Stir the paste into the saucepan, then boil until the mixture thickens. Stir in the remaining cherries, pour into the pastry case, then dot with the melted butter. Cut the remaining pastry into strips 1 cm/½ inch wide. Lay the strips over the filling, crossing to form a lattice. Trim and seal the edges with water. Crimp around the rim, then glaze the top with the beaten egg.

3 Cover the pie with kitchen foil, then bake for 30 minutes in the oven. Remove from the oven, discard the foil, then bake for a further 15 minutes, or until golden. Serve with ice cream.

★ **Variation**

Blueberries and cherries work well together. Add some fresh or frozen blueberries to the filling or serve alongside the ice cream.

GRANDMA'S BEST BAKES

VANILLA CUPCAKES

Makes: 12

Prep: 30 mins, plus cooling

Cook: 15–20 mins

Ingredients

175 g/6 oz unsalted butter, softened

175 g/6 oz caster sugar

3 large eggs, beaten

1 tsp vanilla extract

175 g/6 oz self-raising flour

Icing

150 g/5½ oz unsalted butter, softened

3 tbsp double cream or milk

1 tsp vanilla extract

300 g/10½ oz icing sugar, sifted

hundreds and thousands, to decorate

Method

1 Preheat the oven to 180°C/350°F/Gas Mark 4. Place 12 paper cases in a bun tin.

2 Put the butter and caster sugar into a bowl and whisk together until pale and creamy. Gradually whisk in the eggs and vanilla extract. Sift in the flour and fold in gently.

3 Divide the mixture evenly between the paper cases and bake in the preheated oven for 15–20 minutes, or until risen and firm to the touch. Transfer to a wire rack and leave to cool.

4 To make the icing, put the butter into a bowl and whisk with an electric whisk for 2–3 minutes, or until pale and creamy. Whisk in the cream and vanilla extract. Gradually whisk in the icing sugar and continue whisking until the buttercream is light and fluffy.

5 Use a palette knife to swirl the icing over the top of the cupcakes. Decorate with the hundreds and thousands.

★ Variation

To make bite-size cupcakes for children's parties, divide the batter among 30 mini cupcake liners and reduce the cooking time to 8–10 minutes.

GRANDMA'S BEST BAKES

CHERRY CAKE

Serves: 8

Prep: 30 mins,
plus cooling

Cook: 1–1¼ hrs

Ingredients

250 g/9 oz glacé cherries,
quartered

85 g/3 oz ground almonds

200 g/7 oz plain flour

1 tsp baking powder

200 g/7 oz unsalted butter,
plus extra for greasing

200 g/7 oz caster sugar

3 large eggs

finely grated rind and juice
of 1 lemon

6 sugar cubes, crushed

Method

1 Preheat the oven to 180°C/350°F/Gas Mark 4.
Grease a 20-cm/8-inch round cake tin and line
with baking paper.

2 Stir together the cherries, almonds and 1
tablespoon of the flour. Sift together the
remaining flour and the baking powder into a
separate bowl.

3 Cream together the butter and sugar until light
and fluffy. Gradually add the eggs, whisking hard
until evenly mixed.

4 Add the flour mixture and fold lightly and evenly
into the creamed mixture with a metal spoon.
Add the cherry mixture, fold in evenly, then fold
the lemon rind and juice.

5 Spoon the mixture into the prepared tin and sprinkle
with the crushed sugar cubes. Bake in the preheated
oven for 1–1¼ hours or until risen and golden brown
and shrinking from the sides of the tin.

6 Leave to cool in the tin for about 15 minutes, then
turn out on to a wire rack to cool completely.

LAVENDER SHORTBREAD

Serves: 8

Prep: 25–30 mins, plus chilling and cooling

Cook: 30–35 mins

Ingredients

115 g/4 oz butter, softened, plus extra for greasing

55 g/2 oz lavender caster sugar, plus extra for sprinkling

140 g/5 oz plain flour

25 g/1 oz cornflour

Method

1 Preheat the oven to 160°C/325°F/Gas Mark 3. Lightly grease a baking sheet. Place the butter in a bowl. Sift over the caster sugar (reserving the lavender flowers left in the sieve) and beat together with a wooden spoon until light and fluffy.

2 Sift over the flour and cornflour and add the reserved lavender. Gradually work the flours into the creamed mixture to form a crumbly dough. Gather the dough together with your hands and knead lightly until smooth. Wrap the dough in clingfilm and chill in the refrigerator for 20 minutes.

3 Place the dough on the baking sheet and, using clean hands, press it out to an 18-cm/7-inch circle. Smooth the top by gently rolling a rolling pin over the mixture a couple of times. Crimp around the edge and mark into eight triangles with a sharp knife. Sprinkle with a little more lavender sugar. Chill in the refrigerator for at least 30 minutes until firm. Bake in the preheated oven for 30–35 minutes until just pale golden. Leave the shortbread on the sheet for 10 minutes, then transfer to a wire rack to cool completely.

SCONES

Makes: 12

Prep: 25 mins,
plus cooling

Cook: 10–12 mins

Ingredients

450 g/1 lb plain flour,
plus extra for dusting

½ tsp salt

2 tsp baking powder

55 g/2 oz butter

2 tbsp caster sugar

250 ml/9 fl oz milk

3 tbsp milk, for glazing

strawberry jam and clotted
cream, to serve

Method

1 Preheat the oven to 220°C/425°F/Gas Mark 7. Lightly
flour or line a baking sheet with baking paper.

2 Sift the flour, salt and baking powder into a bowl.
Rub in the butter until the mixture resembles
breadcrumbs. Stir in the sugar. Make a well in the
centre and pour in the milk. Stir in using a round-
bladed knife and make a soft dough.

3 Turn the mixture onto a floured surface and lightly
flatten the dough until it is of an even thickness,
about 1 cm/½ inch. Don't be heavy handed,
scones need a light touch.

4 Use a 6-cm/2½-inch pastry cutter to cut out the
scones and place on the prepared baking sheet.
Glaze with a little milk and bake in the preheated
oven for 10–12 minutes, until golden and well
risen. Cool on a wire rack and serve freshly
baked, with strawberry jam and clotted cream.

RHUBARB, RAISIN & GINGER MUFFINS

Makes: 12

Prep: 25 mins, plus cooling

Cook: 20–25 mins

Ingredients

oil or melted butter, for greasing (if using)

250 g/9 oz rhubarb

200 g/7 oz plain flour

2 tsp baking powder

115 g/4 oz caster sugar

2 eggs

100 ml/3½ fl oz milk

125 g/4½ oz butter, melted and cooled

3 tbsp raisins

2 pieces of stem ginger in syrup, drained and chopped

Method

1 Preheat the oven to 180°C/350°F/Gas Mark 4. Grease a 12-cup muffin tin or line with 12 paper cases. Chop the rhubarb into 1-cm/½-inch lengths

2 Sift together the flour and baking powder into a large bowl. Stir in the sugar. Lightly beat the eggs in a large jug, then beat in the milk and melted butter. Make a well in the centre of the dry ingredients and pour in the beaten liquid ingredients. Stir in the rhubarb, raisins and stem ginger until just combined; do not over-mix.

3 Spoon the mixture into the prepared muffin tin. Bake in the preheated oven for 15–20 minutes, until well risen, golden brown and firm to the touch.

4 Leave the muffins in the tin for 5 minutes, then serve warm or transfer to a wire rack and leave to cool.

CLASSIC OATMEAL COOKIES

Makes: 30

Prep: 20–25 mins, plus cooling

Cook: 15 mins

Ingredients

175 g/6 oz butter, softened, plus extra for greasing

275 g/9¾ oz demerara sugar

1 egg, beaten

4 tbsp water

1 tsp vanilla extract

375 g/13 oz rolled oats

140 g/5 oz plain flour

1 tsp salt

½ tsp bicarbonate of soda

Method

1 Preheat the oven to 180°C/350°F/Gas Mark 4. Grease two large baking sheets.

2 Place the butter and sugar in a large bowl and beat together until pale and creamy. Beat in the egg, water and vanilla extract until the mixture is smooth. Mix the oats, flour, salt and bicarbonate of soda together in a separate bowl, then gradually stir the oat mixture into the creamed mixture until thoroughly combined.

3 Place tablespoonfuls of the mixture on the prepared baking sheets, spaced well apart.

4 Bake in the preheated oven for 15 minutes, or until golden brown. Transfer to wire racks to cool completely.

GRANDMA'S BEST BAKES

GINGERNUTS

Makes: 30

Prep: 25–30 mins, plus cooling

Cook: 20–25 mins

Ingredients

0 g/12 oz self-raising flour

pinch of salt

200 g/7 oz caster sugar

1 tbsp ground ginger

tsp bicarbonate of soda

125 g/4½ oz butter, plus extra for greasing

75 g/2¾ oz golden syrup

1 egg, beaten

1 tsp grated orange rind

Method

1 Preheat the oven to 160°C/325°F/Gas Mark 3. Lightly grease several baking sheets.

2 Sift together the flour, salt, sugar, ginger and bicarbonate of soda into a large mixing bowl.

3 Heat the butter and golden syrup together in a saucepan over a very low heat until the butter has melted. Remove the pan from the heat and leave to cool slightly, then pour the contents onto the dry ingredients.

4 Add the egg and orange rind and mix thoroughly with a wooden spoon to form a dough. Using your hands, carefully shape the dough into 30 even-sized balls. Place the balls on the prepared baking sheets, spaced well apart, then flatten them slightly with your fingers.

5 Bake in the preheated oven for 15–20 minutes, then carefully transfer to a wire racks to cool completely.

ICED MADEIRA CAKE

Serves: 10

Prep: 35 mins,
plus cooling and setting

Cook: 1–1¼ hours

Ingredients

175 g/6 oz unsalted butter, softened, plus extra for greasing

175 g/6 oz caster sugar

finely grated rind of 1 lemon

3 eggs, lightly beaten

140 g/5 oz self-raising flour

115 g/4 oz plain flour

2 tbsp milk

1 tbsp lemon juice

Icing

175 g/6 oz icing sugar

2–3 tbsp lemon juice

2 tsp lemon curd, warmed

Method

1 Preheat the oven to 160°C/325°F/Gas Mark 3. Grease a 900-g/2-lb loaf tin and line with baking paper.

2 Place the butter and caster sugar in a large bowl and beat together until very pale and fluffy. Beat in the lemon rind then gradually beat in the eggs.

3 Sift the self-raising and plain flour into the mixture and fold in gently until thoroughly incorporated. Fold in the milk and lemon juice.

4 Spoon the mixture into the prepared tin and bake in the preheated oven for 1–1¼ hours, or until well risen, golden brown and a skewer inserted into the centre comes out clean. Cool in the tin for 15 minutes, then turn out onto a wire rack to cool completely.

5 For the icing, sift the icing sugar into a bowl. Add the lemon juice and stir to make a smooth and thick icing. Gently spread the icing over the top of the cake. Drizzle the warmed lemon curd over the icing and drag a skewer through the icing to create a swirled effect. Leave to set.

IRISH SPICED FRUIT CAKE

Serves: 8–10

Prep: 25 mins, plus cooling

Cook: 2 hours 10 mins

Ingredients

225 g/8 oz mixed dried fruit, such as sultanas, currants and raisins

100 g/3½ oz dried unsweetened cherries

40 g/1½ oz walnuts, roughly chopped

150 g/5½ oz demerara sugar

115 g/4 oz butter, plus extra for greasing

1 tsp mixed spice

1 tsp ground ginger

½ tsp bicarbonate of soda

225 ml/8 fl oz milk

225 g/8 oz self-raising flour

2 eggs, lightly beaten

Method

1 Put all the ingredients apart from the flour and eggs into a saucepan and mix well. Bring to the boil over a medium–high heat, stirring constantly. Reduce the heat slightly and simmer for 5 minutes, stirring occasionally. Remove from the heat and leave to cool for about 30 minutes.

2 Meanwhile, preheat the oven to 180°C/350°F/Gas Mark 4. Grease and line a deep 20-cm/8-inch cake tin.

3 Add the flour and eggs to the cake mixture, mixing well to combine. Spoon the mixture into the prepared tin, levelling the surface with a wet palette knife.

4 Bake in the preheated oven for 30 minutes. Reduce the oven temperature to 160°C/325°F/Gas Mark 3 and bake for a further 1½ hours, or until a skewer inserted in the centre comes out clean.

5 Leave the cake to cool in the tin for 10 minutes then turn out on to a wire rack and leave to cool completely.

CUSTARD TARTS

Makes: 12

Prep: 40–45 mins, plus cooling

Cook: 30 mins

Ingredients

butter, for greasing

5 egg yolks, lightly beaten

100 g/3½ oz caster sugar

2 tsp cornflour

125 ml/4 fl oz full fat milk

250 ml/9 fl oz double cream

5-cm/2-inch cinnamon stick

2 strips orange peel

½ tsp vanilla extract

375 g/13 oz pre-rolled puff pastry

freshly grated nutmeg, for sprinkling

flour, for dusting

Method

1 Preheat the oven to 190°C/375°F/Gas Mark 5. Lightly grease a 12-hole muffin tin. Combine the egg yolks and sugar in a mixing bowl. Stir in the cornflour and mix to a smooth paste, then whisk in the milk.

2 Heat the cream in a heavy-based saucepan until just starting to simmer but not boiling. Gradually whisk the hot cream into the egg mixture, then return the mixture to the pan. Add the cinnamon stick and orange peel. Whisk constantly over a medium heat for about 5 minutes, until thickened. Immediately pour into a jug. Stir in the vanilla extract. Cover with clingfilm to prevent a skin forming and set aside.

3 Place the sheet of puff pastry on a board and trim to a rectangle measuring about 28 x 24 cm/11 x 9½ inches (weighing about 300 g/10½ oz). Discard the trimmings or use in another recipe. Slice in half lengthways to make two rectangles, each measuring 28 x 12 cm/11 x 4½ inches. Sprinkle one rectangle with freshly grated nutmeg. Place the other on top to make a sandwich. Roll up from the narrow end to make a log. Using a sharp knife, cut the log into twelve 1-cm/½-inch slices.

Roll out the slices on a floured board to 12-cm/4½-inch rounds. Place the rounds in the muffin-tin holes, lightly pressing down into the base and leaving a slightly thicker rim round the top edge.

Remove the cinnamon stick and orange peel from the custard and discard. Pour the custard into the pastry cases.

Bake for 20 minutes, or until the pastry and filling are golden brown. Leave the tarts to cool in the tin for 5 minutes, then transfer to a wire rack to cool.

COFFEE & WALNUT CAKE

Serves: 8 **Prep: 35 mins,** plus cooling **Cook: 20–25 mins**

Ingredients

175 g/6 oz unsalted butter, softened, plus extra for greasing

175 g/6 oz light muscovado sugar

3 large eggs, beaten

3 tbsp strong black coffee

175 g/6 oz self-raising flour

1½ tsp baking powder

115 g/4 oz walnut pieces

walnut halves, to decorate

Frosting

115 g/4 oz unsalted butter, softened

200 g/7 oz icing sugar

1 tbsp strong black coffee

½ tsp vanilla extract

Method

1 Preheat the oven to 180°C/350°F/Gas Mark 4. Grease two 20-cm/8-inch sandwich tins and line with baking paper.

2 Beat the butter and muscovado sugar together until pale and creamy. Gradually add the eggs, beating well after each addition. Beat in the coffe

3 Sift the flour and baking powder into the mixture, then fold in lightly and evenly with a metal spoon. Fold in the walnut pieces. Divide the mixture between the prepared cake tins and smooth the surfaces. Bake in the preheated oven for 20–25 minutes, or until golden brown and springy to the touch. Turn out onto a wire rack to cool complete

4 To make the frosting, beat together the butter, icing sugar, coffee and vanilla extract, mixing ur smooth and creamy.

5 Use about half the mixture to sandwich the cak together, then spread the remaining frosting on top and swirl with a palette knife. Decorate with walnut halves.

RASPBERRY CRUMBLE MUFFINS

Makes: 12

Prep: 25 mins, plus cooling

Cook: 25 mins

Ingredients

280 g/10 oz plain flour

1 tbsp baking powder

½ tsp bicarbonate of soda

pinch of salt

115 g/4 oz caster sugar

2 eggs

250 ml/9 fl oz natural yogurt

85 g/3 oz butter, melted and cooled, plus extra for greasing

1 tsp vanilla extract

150 g/5½ oz frozen raspberries

Crumble topping

50 g/1¾ oz plain flour

35 g/1¼ oz butter

25 g/1 oz caster sugar

Method

1 Preheat the oven to 200°C/400°F/Gas Mark 6. Grease a 12-hole muffin tin or line with 12 paper cases.

2 To make the crumble topping, sift the flour into a bowl. Cut the butter into small pieces, add to the bowl with the flour and rub it in with your fingertips until the mixture resembles fine breadcrumbs. Stir in the sugar and set aside.

3 To make the muffins, sift together the flour, baking powder, bicarbonate of soda and salt into a large bowl. Stir in the sugar.

4 Lightly whisk the eggs in a large bowl, then whisk in the yogurt, butter and vanilla extract. Make a well in the centre of the dry ingredients, pour in the beaten liquid ingredients and add the raspberries. Stir gently until just combined. Do not over-mix.

5 Spoon the mixture into the prepared tin. Scatter the crumble topping over each muffin and press down lightly. Bake in the preheated oven for about 20 minutes until well risen, golden brown and firm to the touch.

6 Leave the muffins to cool in the tin for 5 minutes, then serve warm or transfer to a wire rack to cool completely.

GRANDMA'S BEST BAKES

CHOCOLATE CARAMEL SHORTBREAD

Makes: 12 pieces approx.

Prep: 25–30 mins, plus chilling

Cook: 25–30 mins

Ingredients

115 g/4 oz butter, plus extra for greasing

175 g/6 oz plain flour

55 g/2 oz golden caster sugar

Filling & Topping

175 g/6 oz butter

115 g/4 oz golden caster sugar

3 tbsp golden syrup

400 g/14 oz canned condensed milk

00 g/7 oz plain chocolate, broken into pieces

Method

1 Preheat the oven to 180°C/350°F/Gas Mark 4. Grease and line a 23-cm/9-inch shallow square cake tin with baking paper.

2 Place the butter, flour and sugar in a food processor and process until it begins to bind together. Press the mixture into the prepared tin and smooth the top. Bake in the preheated oven for 20–25 minutes.

3 Meanwhile, make the filling. Place the butter, sugar, golden syrup and condensed milk in a saucepan and heat gently until the sugar has dissolved. Bring to the boil and simmer for 6–8 minutes, stirring constantly, until the mixture becomes very thick. Pour over the shortbread base and leave to chill in the refrigerator until firm.

4 To make the topping, place the chocolate in a heatproof bowl, set the bowl over a saucepan of gently simmering water and heat until melted, then spread over the caramel. Chill in the refrigerator until set. Cut the shortbread into 12 pieces with a sharp knife and serve.

GRANDMA'S BEST BAKES

LEMON BUTTERFLY CUPCAKES

Makes: 12

Prep: 30 mins, plus cooling

Cook: 15–20 mins

Ingredients

115 g/4 oz self-raising flour
½ tsp baking powder
115 g/4 oz butter, softened
115 g/4 oz caster sugar
2 eggs, beaten
finely grated rind of ¾ lemon
2–4 tbsp milk
icing sugar, for dusting

Filling
55 g/2 oz butter
115 g/4 oz icing sugar
1 tbsp lemon juice

Method

1 Preheat the oven to 190°C/375°F/Gas Mark 5. Place 12 paper cases in a bun tin.

2 Sift the flour and baking powder into a bowl. Add the butter, caster sugar, eggs, lemon rind and enough milk to give a medium-soft consistency. Beat the mixture thoroughly until smooth, then divide between the paper cases.

3 Bake in the preheated oven for 15–20 minutes, or until well risen and golden. Transfer to a wire rack to cool.

4 To make the filling, place the butter in a bowl. Sift in the icing sugar and add the lemon juice. Beat well until smooth and creamy.

5 When the cakes are completely cooled, use a sharp-pointed vegetable knife to cut a circle from the top of each cake, then cut each circle in half. Spoon a little buttercream filling on top of each cake and press the two semi-circular pieces into it to resemble wings. Dust the cakes with icing sugar before serving.

GRANDMA'S BEST BAKES

CHOCOLATE & CHERRY BROWNIES

Makes: 12

Prep: 25 mins, plus cooling

Cook: 50-55 mins

Ingredients

5 g/6 oz plain chocolate, broken into pieces

175 g/6 oz butter, plus extra for greasing

225 g/8 oz caster sugar

3 large eggs, beaten

1 tsp vanilla extract

5 g/4½ oz self-raising flour

175 g/6 oz fresh cherries, stoned

5 g/3 oz white chocolate, roughly chopped

Method

1. Preheat the oven to 180°C/350°F/Gas Mark 4. Grease a 24 x 20-cm/9½ x 8-inch shallow cake tin and line with baking paper.

2. Put the plain chocolate and butter into a large, heatproof bowl set over a saucepan of simmering water and heat until melted. Remove from the heat and leave to cool for 5 minutes.

3. Beat the sugar, eggs and vanilla extract into the chocolate mixture. Sift in the flour and fold in gently. Pour the mixture into the prepared tin. Scatter over the cherries and the white chocolate.

4. Bake in the preheated oven for 30 minutes. Loosely cover the tops of the brownies with foil and bake for a further 15-20 minutes, or until just firm to the touch. Leave to cool in the tin, then cut into pieces.

GRANDMA'S BEST BAKES

DATE & WALNUT LOAF

Makes: 1 loaf

Prep: 25 mins, plus soaking and cooling

Cook: 35–40 mins

Ingredients

100 g/3½ oz dates, stoned and chopped

½ tsp bicarbonate of soda

finely grated rind of ½ lemon

100 ml/3½ fl oz hot tea

40 g/1½ oz unsalted butter, plus extra for greasing

70 g/2½ oz light muscovado sugar

1 small egg

125 g/4½ oz self-raising flour

25 g/1 oz walnuts, chopped

walnut halves, to decorate

Method

1 Preheat the oven to 180°C/350°F/Gas Mark 4. Grease a 450-g/1-lb loaf tin and line with baking paper.

2 Place the dates, bicarbonate of soda and lemon rind in a bowl and add the hot tea. Leave to soak for 10 minutes until softened.

3 Cream the butter and sugar together until light and fluffy, then beat in the egg. Stir in the date mixture.

4 Fold in the flour using a large metal spoon, then fold in the walnuts. Spoon the mixture into the prepared cake tin and smooth the surface. Top with the walnut halves.

5 Bake in the preheated oven for 35–40 minutes or until risen, firm and golden brown. Cool for 10 minutes in the tin, then turn out onto a wire rack to cool completely.

WHOLEMEAL MUFFINS

Makes: 10

Prep: 25 mins,
plus cooling

Cook: 25–30 mins

Ingredients

225 g/8 oz self-raising
wholemeal flour

2 tsp baking powder

25 g/1 oz light
muscovado sugar

100 g/3½ oz ready-to-eat
dried apricots,
finely chopped

1 banana, mashed with
1 tbsp orange juice

1 tsp orange rind,
finely grated

300 ml/10 fl oz skimmed milk

1 egg, beaten

3 tbsp corn oil

2 tbsp porridge oats

fruit spread, honey or maple
syrup, to serve

Method

1 Preheat the oven to 200°C/400°F/Gas Mark 6.
Place 10 paper muffin cases in a muffin tin. Sift
the flour and baking powder into a mixing bowl,
adding any husks that remain in the sieve. Stir in
the sugar and chopped apricots.

2 Make a well in the centre of the dry ingredients
and add the banana, orange rind, milk, beaten
egg and oil. Mix together well to form a thick
batter. Divide the batter evenly among the 10
paper cases.

3 Sprinkle each muffin with a few porridge oats
and bake in the preheated oven for 25–30
minutes, or until well risen and firm to the touch.
Transfer the muffins to a wire rack to cool slightly.
Serve the muffins warm with a little fruit spread.

PORTER CAKE

Makes: one 7-inch cake

Prep: 35 mins, plus soaking, cooling & storing

Cook: 2¼-3 hours

Ingredients

450 g/1 lb mixed currants and sultanas

115 g/4 oz dried unsweetened cherries

115 g/4 oz mixed citrus peel, finely chopped

325 ml/11 fl oz stout

350 g/12 oz plain flour

1 tsp baking powder

1 tsp mixed spice

pinch of salt

225 g/8 oz butter, plus extra for greasing

225 g/8 oz soft brown sugar

3 eggs, lightly beaten

Method

1 Mix the currants, sultanas, cherries and citrus peel in a large bowl. Add the stout and leave to soak for at least 5 hours or overnight, stirring occasionally.

2 Preheat the oven to 160°C/325°F/Gas Mark 3. Grease and line an 18-cm/7-inch square cake tin. Sift the flour, baking powder, spice and salt into a large bowl.

3 Cream the butter and sugar in a separate bowl for about 4 minutes, until light and fluffy. Stir in the beaten eggs, a little at a time, adding some of the flour mixture at each addition and beating well. Stir in the remaining flour.

4 Add the fruit and any liquid to the mixture, mixing well to a soft consistency. Spoon the mixture into the prepared tin, levelling the surface with a wet palette knife.

5 Bake in the preheated oven for 1 hour. Reduce the oven temperature to 150°C/300°F/Gas Mark 2 and bake for a further 1½-2 hours, or until a skewer inserted in the centre comes out clean. Leave in the tin until completely cool.

6 Turn out, wrap in greaseproof paper and store in an airtight container.

CORNBREAD

Makes: 1 loaf

Prep: 25 mins,
plus cooling

Cook: 30–35 mins

Ingredients

vegetable oil, for greasing
175 g/6 oz plain flour
1 tsp salt
4 tsp baking powder
1 tsp caster sugar
280 g/10 oz polenta
115 g/4 oz butter, softened
4 eggs
250 ml/9 fl oz milk
3 tbsp double cream

Method

1 Preheat the oven to 200°C/400°F/Gas Mark 6. Brush a 20-cm/8-inch square cake tin with oil.

2 Sift the flour, salt and baking powder together into a bowl. Add the sugar and polenta and stir to mix. Add the butter and cut into the dry ingredients with a knife, then rub it in with your fingertips until the mixture resembles fine breadcrumbs.

3 Lightly whisk the eggs in a bowl with the milk and cream, then stir into the polenta mixture until thoroughly combined.

4 Spoon the mixture into the prepared tin and smooth the surface. Bake in the preheated oven for 30–35 minutes, until a wooden cocktail stick inserted into the centre of the loaf comes out clean. Remove the tin from the oven and leave to cool for 5–10 minutes, then cut into squares and serve warm.

ENGLISH MUFFINS

Makes: 10-12

Prep: 35-40 mins, plus **Cook: 30-35 mins**
rising and optional cooling

Ingredients

450 g/1 lb strong white flour,
plus extra for dusting

½ tsp salt

1 tsp caster sugar

1½ tsp easy-blend
dried yeast

250 ml/9 fl oz
lukewarm water

125 ml/4 fl oz natural yogurt

vegetable oil, for oiling

40 g/1½ oz semolina

butter and jam, to serve

Method

1 Sift the flour and salt together into a bowl and stir in the sugar and yeast. Make a well in the centre and add the water and yogurt. Stir with a wooden spoon until the dough begins to come together, then knead until it comes away from the side of the bowl. Turn out onto a lightly floured surface and knead for 5–10 minutes, until smooth and elastic.

2 Brush a bowl with oil. Shape the dough into a ball, put it in the bowl and cover with a damp tea towel. Leave to rise in a warm place for 30–40 minutes, until the dough has doubled in volume. Dust a baking tray with flour. Turn out the dough onto a lightly floured surface and knead lightly. Roll out to a thickness of 2 cm/¾ inch. Stamp out 10–12 rounds with a 7.5-cm/3-inch biscuit cutter and sprinkle each round with semolina. Place on the baking tray, cover with a damp tea towel and leave to rise in a warm place for 30–40 minutes.

3 Heat a griddle or large frying pan over a medium–high heat and brush lightly with oil. Add half the muffins and cook for 7–8 minutes on each side, until golden brown. Cook the remaining muffins in the same way. Serve hot with butter and jam or cool, then split and toast them before serving.

★ Variation

Add 1 tbsp of cinnamon to step 1 for a delicious twist.

BROWN SODA BREAD WITH TREACLE

Makes: 1 loaf

Prep: 20 mins, plus cooling

Cook: 35–40 mins

Ingredients

250 g/9 oz plain flour, plus extra for dusting

250 g/9 oz wholemeal flour

50 g/1¾ oz jumbo oat flakes

1½ tsp salt

1 tsp bicarbonate of soda

400 ml/14 fl oz buttermilk

2 tbsp black treacle

Method

1 Preheat the oven to 230°C/450°F/Gas Mark 8. Line a baking tray with a sheet of non-stick baking paper.

2 Combine the flours, oats, salt and bicarbonate of soda in a large bowl, mixing thoroughly.

3 Whisk together the buttermilk and treacle in a large jug. Make a well in the centre of the flour mixture and pour in the buttermilk mixture. Using a fork, stir the liquid, gradually drawing in the flour from around the edge. With floured hands, lightly knead to a soft dough.

4 Shape the dough into a round and place on the lined baking tray. Press flat to about 5 cm/2 inches thick. Use a sharp knife with a long blade to cut a deep cross on the top.

5 Bake in the preheated oven for 15 minutes, then reduce the oven temperature to 200°C/400°F/ Gas Mark 6. Bake for a further 20–25 minutes, or until the base of the bread sounds hollow when tapped. Transfer to a wire rack and leave to cool slightly. Serve warm.

TREACLE BREAD

Makes: 1 loaf

Prep: 30 mins, plus cooling

Cook: 45–55 mins

Ingredients

225 g/8 oz plain flour

1 tsp bicarbonate of soda

½ tsp mixed spice

½ tsp ground ginger

60 g/2¼ oz lightly salted butter, plus extra for greasing and to serve

3 tbsp treacle

2 eggs, lightly beaten

80 ml/3 fl oz buttermilk

50 g/1¾ oz soft brown sugar

50 g/1¾ oz currants

50 g/1¾ oz sultanas

Method

1 Preheat the oven to 180°C/350°F/Gas Mark 4. Grease and line a small 17 x 9.5-cm/6½ x 3¼-inch loaf tin.

2 Sift the flour, bicarbonate of soda and spices into a bowl. Lightly rub in the butter until the mixture resembles fine breadcrumbs.

3 Whisk the treacle with the eggs and buttermilk, then stir in the sugar. Make a well in the centre of the flour mixture and pour in the treacle mixture. Mix with a fork, gradually drawing in the flour from around the edges.

4 Add the currants and sultanas, and mix to a soft dough. Spoon the dough into the prepared loaf tin, levelling the surface with a wet palette knife.

5 Bake in the preheated oven for 45–55 minutes, or until a skewer inserted in the centre comes out clean.

6 Leave to cool in the tin for 15 minutes, then turn out onto a wire rack and leave for about 2 hours to cool completely.

7 Serve spread thickly with butter.

SAVOURY OAT CRACKERS

Makes: 12–14

Prep: 25–30 mins, plus cooling

Cook: 12–15 mins

Ingredients

100 g/3½ oz unsalted butter, plus extra for greasing

90 g/3¼ oz rolled oats

25 g/1 oz plain wholemeal flour

½ tsp coarse sea salt

1 tsp dried thyme

40 g/1½ oz walnuts, finely chopped

1 egg, beaten

40 g/1½ oz sesame seeds

Method

1 Preheat the oven to 180°C/350°F/Gas Mark 4. Lightly grease two baking trays.

2 Rub the butter into the oats and flour using your fingertips. Stir in the salt, thyme and walnuts, then add the egg and mix to a soft dough. Spread out the sesame seeds on a large shallow plate or tray. Break off walnut-sized pieces of dough and roll into balls, then roll in the sesame seeds to coat lightly and evenly.

3 Place the balls of dough on the prepared baking trays, spacing well apart, and roll the rolling pin over them to flatten. Bake in the preheated oven for 12–15 minutes, or until firm and pale golden. Transfer to a wire rack and leave to cool.

GRANDMA'S BEST BAKES

SEEDED BREAD ROLLS

Makes: 8

Prep: 30 mins,
plus rising and cooling

Cook: 10–15 mins

Ingredients

50 g/1 lb strong white flour,
plus extra for dusting

1 tsp salt

7 g/¼ oz easy-blend dried
yeast

1 tbsp vegetable oil,
plus extra for brushing

350 ml/12 fl oz
lukewarm water

1 egg, beaten

sesame or poppy seeds,
for sprinkling

Method

1 Place the flour, salt and yeast in a large bowl and mix well. Pour in the oil and add the water, then mix well to make a smooth dough.

2 Turn out onto a lightly floured surface and knead well for 5–7 minutes, or until smooth and elastic. Brush a bowl with oil. Shape the dough into a ball, place it in the bowl and cover with a damp tea towel. Leave to rise in a warm place for 1 hour, or until the dough has doubled in volume.

3 Turn out the dough onto a lightly floured surface and knead briefly until smooth. Divide the dough into eight pieces. Shape half the dough into round rolls. Make the other half into cottage rolls with a small round shape on top. Place the rolls on a baking sheet.

4 Cover the rolls with a damp tea towel and leave to rise for 30 minutes, or until the rolls have doubled in size.

5 Preheat the oven to 220°C/425°F/Gas Mark 7. Brush the rolls with the beaten egg and sprinkle with seeds. Bake in the preheated oven for 10–15 minutes, or until golden brown. Test that the rolls are cooked by tapping on the bases with your knuckles – they should sound hollow. Transfer to a wire rack to cool.

GRANDMA'S BEST BAKES

GRANARY LOAF

Makes: 1 loaf

Prep: 25 mins,
plus rising and cooling

Cook: 30–35 mins

Ingredients

500 g/1 lb 2 oz granary flour, plus extra for dusting

1½ tsp salt

2 tsp fast action dried yeast

2 tsp sunflower seeds

1 tbsp sunflower oil, plus extra for greasing

1 tsp runny honey

300 ml/10 fl oz warm water

Method

1 Mix the granary flour, salt, yeast and the sunflower seeds in a large bowl and make a well in the centre. Mix together the oil, honey and warm water and pour into the bowl. Mix with a knife to make a soft, sticky dough.

2 Turn the dough onto a floured surface and knead for 10 minutes until smooth and elastic, adding a little more flour if the dough becomes too sticky. Place in a bowl, cover with lightly oiled clingfilm and leave in a warm place for 1–1½ hours until doubled in size. Preheat the oven to 220°C/425°F/ Gas Mark 7. Lightly grease a 900-g/2-lb loaf tin.

3 Turn the dough onto a floured surface and knead again lightly for 1 minute. Shape into an oblong and place in the loaf tin. Cover with a clean damp tea towel and leave in a warm place for about 30 minutes until the dough has risen above the top of the edges of the tin. Dust the top of the loaf lightly with flour. Bake in the preheated oven for 30–35 minutes until golden brown and the loaf sounds hollow when tapped on the base with your knuckles. Transfer to a wire rack to cool.

SEEDED RYE BREAD

Makes: 1 loaf

Prep: 25–30 mins,
plus rising and cooling

Cook: 35–40 mins

Ingredients

250 g/9 oz rye flour,
plus extra for dusting

250 g/9 oz
strong white flour

1½ tsp salt

1 tbsp caraway seeds

7 g/¼ oz easy-blend
dried yeast

25 g/1 oz butter, melted

2 tbsp honey, warmed

300 ml/10 fl oz
lukewarm water

sunflower oil, for greasing

Method

1 Mix the rye flour, white flour, salt, caraway seeds
   and yeast in a large bowl and make a well in the
   centre. Mix together the butter, honey and water
   and pour into the well. Mix with a knife to make a
   soft, sticky dough. Lightly grease a baking sheet
   with oil.

2 Turn out the dough onto a floured work surface
   and knead for 10 minutes, or until smooth and
   elastic. Shape into an oval and place on the
   prepared baking sheet. Slash the top of the loaf
   in a diamond pattern, lightly dust with flour and
   leave in a warm place for 1–1½ hours, or until
   doubled in size.

3 Meanwhile, preheat the oven to 190°C/375°F/
   Gas Mark 5. Bake in the preheated oven for 30–
   35 minutes, or until the crust is a rich brown colour
   and the base of the loaf sounds hollow when
   tapped with your knuckles. Transfer to a wire rack
   to cool.

OAT & POTATO BREAD

Makes: 1 loaf

Prep: 30–35 mins, plus cooling and rising

Cook: 50–60 mins

Ingredients

vegetable oil, for oiling

225 g/8 oz floury potatoes (peeled weight)

500 g/1 lb 2 oz strong white flour, plus extra for dusting

1½ tsp salt

40 g/1½ oz butter, diced

1½ tsp easy-blend dried yeast

1½ tbsp soft dark brown sugar

3 tbsp rolled oats

2 tbsp skimmed milk powder

210 ml/7½ fl oz lukewarm water

Topping

1 tbsp water

1 tbsp rolled oats

Method

1 Oil a 900-g/2-lb loaf tin. Put the potatoes in a large saucepan, add water to cover and bring to the boil. Cook for 20–25 minutes, until tender. Drain, then mash until smooth. Leave to cool.

2 Sift the flour and salt into a warmed bowl. Rub in the butter with your fingertips. Stir in the yeast, sugar, oats and milk powder. Mix in the mashed potato, then add the water and mix to a soft dough.

3 Turn out the dough onto a lightly floured work surface and knead for 5–10 minutes, or until smooth and elastic. Put the dough in an oiled bowl, cover with clingfilm and leave to rise in a warm place for 1 hour, or until doubled in size.

4 Turn out the dough again and knead lightly. Shape into a loaf and transfer to the prepared tin. Cover and leave to rise in a warm place for 30 minutes. Meanwhile, preheat the oven to 220°C/425°F/Gas Mark 7.

5 Brush the surface of the loaf with the water and carefully sprinkle over the oats. Bake in the preheated oven for 25–30 minutes, or until it sounds hollow when tapped on the bottom. Transfer to a wire rack and leave to cool slightly. Serve warm.

★ **Variation**

For a starter spread cream cheese on slices then top with smoked salmon and a squeeze of lemon juice.

GRANDMA'S BEST BAKES

INDEX

This edition published by Parragon Books Ltd in 2015
LOVE FOOD is an imprint of Parragon Books Ltd

Parragon Books Ltd
Chartist House
15–17 Trim Street
Bath BA1 1HA, UK
www.parragon.com/lovefood

ISBN 978-1-4723-9245-9
Printed in China

Introduction by Anne Sheasby
Front cover photography by Ian Garlick
Cover food stylist Nikki Gee

Notes for the Reader
This book uses both metric and imperial measurements. Follow the
same units of measurement throughout; do not mix metric and imperial.
All spoon measurements are level: teaspoons are assumed to be 5 ml,
and tablespoons are assumed to be 15 ml. Unless otherwise stated, milk
is assumed to be full fat, eggs and individual vegetables are medium,
and pepper is freshly ground black pepper and salt is table salt. Unless
otherwise stated, all root vegetables should be peeled prior to using.

Garnishes, decorations and serving suggestions are all optional and
not necessarily included in the recipe ingredients or method. The
times given are an approximate guide only. Preparation times differ
according to the techniques used by different people and the cooking
times may also vary from those given. Optional ingredients, variations or
serving suggestions have not been included in the time calculations.

For front cover recipe please see pages 40–41.

BAKING *recipes*

CAKE *recipes*

CHICKEN *recipes*

CUPCAKE & MUFFIN *recipes*

FAST & SIMPLE *recipes*

INDIAN *recipes*

PASTA *recipes*

SLOW COOKER *recipes*

STIR-FRY *recipes*

STUDENT *recipes*

TAPAS *recipes*

VEGETARIAN *recipes*